All in the End is Harvest

All in the End is Harvest

An anthology for those who grieve

Edited by
Agnes Whitaker

Foreword by
Sue MacGregor

Introduction by
Colin Murray Parkes

Published in association with
CRUSE BEREAVEMENT CARE

First published in Great Britain in 1984 by
Darton, Longman and Todd Ltd
1 Spencer Court
140–142 Wandsworth High Street
London SW18 4JJ

in association with

Cruse Bereavement Care
Cruse House
126 Sheen Road
Richmond
Surrey TW9 1UR

Reprinted 2001 (19th printing)

British Library Cataloguing in Publication Data

All in the end is harvest.
 1. Bereavement—Religious aspects—
 Christianity
 I. Whitaker, Agnes   II. CRUSE
 242′.4   BV4905.2

ISBN 0–232–51624–3

Phototypeset by Intype London Ltd
Printed in Great Britain by Page Bros, Norwich

Contents

Foreword

Broadcasters who work on daily, topical programmes, as I do, are privileged people: we meet, we listen to, we ask questions of (in a manner which must sometimes sound downright impertinent) a fascinating selection of our population. In this way I have encountered many bereaved people: mothers whose teenage daughters have died; husbands mourning wives; widows; orphans; parents who have lost a small baby. I have also discussed the psychology of grief with several of the people who appear in this anthology. They all spoke in an admirably helpful and positive way, and by the same token I feel sure that among the many beautiful and moving pieces of writing in this book, anyone who is experiencing a still sharp sense of loss will find words to comfort, and an awareness that their grief is shared and understood by others.

As an anthology of deep feelings and as a tribute to the work of Cruse Bereavement Care it will also be read and appreciated by those who as yet can only guess at what grief will mean to them.

SUE MACGREGOR

Introduction

To a lover of books, libraries are a fearsome blessing – we approach them with awe, conscious of the treasures they contain, but half paralysed by the necessity of choice. In the same way, to a lover of poetry, anthologies are awesome.

We may be tempted to simplify the need for choice by reading them cover to cover, or we may prefer to open the book at random and read on. In either case, we are likely soon to find ourselves suffering from a condition which psychologists have termed 'reactive inhibition', but which is more usually referred to as 'too much of a good thing'.

This anthology is more awesome than most because it treats a species of poetry and prose which most of us find hard to take. Much of the greatest writing is about death and grief, but to concentrate it together under one cover is to expect a lot of the reader – particularly if that reader has been bereaved or come close to death.

Yet these are the very readers who are most likely to seek out a book of this kind. Grief fills the mind and, for a while, it may be difficult to think of anything else. Since grief cannot be avoided, we might as well accept it and find some way to think about it and to make sense of it.

But as every relationship is different, so every grief is different, and we should not expect to find much uniformity in the response to loss or in the solutions which people find to the problems of loss. Words which give comfort to one person may seem like sentimental pap to another. Symbols which to one person are charged with meaning evoke no response in another. Advice which has proved helpful to one person may even harm another.

And yet there is a common chord beneath all this diversity. There are things which most bereaved people have in common, and there are some meanings which emerge again and again in the writings of those who find themselves impelled to write about grief.

One function of poetry is to express emotion, fear, despair, anger, bewilderment, rage – all reflect some aspect of the impact of bereavement. We share the poet's grief and in doing so we make our own grief easier to accept, more real, more earthy, more controlled. A sorrow shared may not reduce that sorrow, but it does remind us we are not alone. Grief is the price we pay for love and we must all be prepared to pay it.

Why should this happen to me, and me, and me? Why not? God never promised you a rose garden. Why should you be exempted from the laws of chance or mischance? Life was never fair.

This book reflects bewilderment and outrage, naked fear and flat despair. It echoes the heartache of disappointed hopes, the agonies of regret and the ugly images which haunt the memory when death comes violent in the night. It is not a comfortable book.

But it also contains positive emotion. Some deaths can be a triumph and some people in the face of loss feel joy and pure delight burst unexpectedly upon their minds. Laughter explodes at the most awkward moments and modern man's capacity for pricking the bubbles of pomp and seeking out hypocrisy shows most keenly in the face of solemn condolence.

Some find the 'peace that passes all understanding' in the successful completion of a life well lived together. Some celebrate the passage of the one they hold most dear from this 'vale of tears' into a better place and time. Some simply feel relief that suffering is done.

It is an arguable question whether these different reactions result from various philosophies of life or whether philosophy itself reflects emotion. Some hold that faith arises from divine enlightenment ('enthusiasm' = to be possessed of gods), others that logical conviction (by the use of scientific method) is the only road; others cynically deride man's objectivity and point out that those beliefs to which we hold most strongly are the ones about which we have least evidence.

The poet struggles with ideas in ways which give offence to logic. Yet there is a truth in poetry and myth that can transcend dry reason. Just as a dream, being the creation of a person's sleeping mind, plays out the meaning of unconscious mental traffic, so the poet plays with symbols in a game whose truth arises from the feelings it contains. How we interpret dream and poem depends on our ability to learn the rules of the game and the meanings of the symbols. And, since poets, like dreamers are inclined to change the rules and to play upon the ambiguities of symbols, the meanings which we glean will be elusive.

Yet there are common themes, ideas of potent imagery and meaning, which emerge again and again throughout this book. One is the theme of hope, hope that, however bad grief may be, it has a meaning; hope that all the good that can come out of love is not lost; hope that the meaning of life extends beyond life.

Another theme is the idea that, however dimly we comprehend it, everything relates to everything else; all is not chaos. Light and shade, pain and pleasure, love and loss are elements of a pattern whose details we perceive, even though we can never hope to perceive the whole. Each one of us is a part, and only a part, of something bigger and more important than ourselves, and that something is ordered by a natural order which is so all-pervading that we find it difficult to name – though some call it 'God'.

And there is another theme which cuts across and includes the others, the theme of transcendence. This is, perhaps, the hardest to contain with words; it struggles and bolts to leap free. It develops out of despair into resignation, from resignation to surrender, from surrender to renunciation, from renunciation to acceptance and from acceptance to transcendence. In this process fear is transmuted into anger and anger into peace.

Death may happen in a moment but grief takes time; and that time is both an ordeal and a blessing. An ordeal. in the sense that grief is often one of the most severe mental pains that we must suffer, and a blessing in the sense that we don't have to do it all at once. We can, to a degree, ration out our grief in bearable dosage; according to our circumstances we may choose to give full vent to grief, and like the Maoris, cry and shout and chant three days and nights on end; or we may stultify our grief, avoiding public show, and leak it, drip by drip, in secret, over many months. But sooner or later, in time, our grief will out, like truth, a harsh reminder of our own mortality.

There are many turning points in the progression of our grief, occasions when events bring home its impact: anniversaries, meetings, recapitulations. At first we think these only serve to aggravate our pain, break down our brittle structures of escape. But, with experience, we learn to treasure them for what they are, reminders of the good things that make up our lives, evidence that 'he (or she) lives on in my memory'. At last it becomes possible to look back with pleasure and look onward now with hope.

This book is a tribute to the work of Cruse Bereavement Care. Cruse is an unlikely body, a group of people with no other aim than to ameliorate the griefs of others. From small beginnings it has grown to offer counsel and support to widows, widowers and their families all over Britain. Those who know Cruse know grief, but they also know compassion and a kind of love – the love which each of us can offer to each other at times of loss. Cruse is an instrument and a symbol of change. We look back at its history with pride, but also with sadness. Many of the people who gave life to Cruse have died; helpers are now bereaved; age and sickness take their toll. But despite these losses, and because of them, the life of Cruse continues. Those who have taken passage through the storms of grief and reached calm waters may return as pilots, and although a major loss is not the only way to know the needs of the bereaved, it adds conviction to the words, 'I understand'. So the bereaved who come for help may stay as helpers, and the cycle is renewed.

And because this book draws on the preferences of those who know Cruse, its choices reflect their experience. Agnes Whitaker has sounded out, enticed, cajoled and gently nagged a necklace of pearls from several beds of oysters, and it is fitting that the former editor of the *Cruse Chronicle* and production editor of *Bereavement Care* should add her own particular favourites. She also makes the reader's task easier by grouping the items into classes and by helpful introductory comments. What emerges is a collection to be savoured slowly over time, not lost upon a shelf but dog-eared by the bedside or in some other private place with bookmarks, paper clips or, dare I say it, pencilled comments in the margin.

DR COLIN MURRAY PARKES OBE
President of Cruse Bereavement Care

Preface

Are not death and grief the most depressing and embarrassing fields to work in? You can sense some acquaintances are thinking that; others actually pluck up courage and say it.

And yet, they are the most challenging fields you can imagine.

Of course there is much heart-aching sadness and anguish, and if you are trying to share a little of it (which is all you can do) then you do take some on board.

But you are also working with some of the most profound, most challenging, most unanswered concepts men and women ever faced, and still face. You are working where medicine and psychiatry meet traditional beliefs, where psychology, religion, theology and philosophy overlap in huge areas, and ideas about the meaning of life and death are expressed in every sort of literature, and every other sort of creative art.

You discover that very many bereaved people find new significance and insight in literature, especially poetry. The certainties that previously rounded many lives have been shattered, and the havoc which grief causes has undermined inner security.

In my work I find that many people have a dormant intuitive understanding of some of the profound philosphical ideas in our lives and deaths, which for various reasons may normally not have the opportunity to surface. I think bereavement can perforce provide that opportunity; many have a remarkable new openness to deep ideas and images, especially in poetry. If they do not follow this up, then I think the door gradually closes again, as everything fades into the light of common day. But if, during a period of grieving, you dig deeply into literature, about God or providence, about whether there is a purpose in our lives and a meaning in our deaths, about the natural world, about relationships with fellow humans – then I think you can be altered for ever. Whatever particular conclusions you come to, I believe most pilgrims or seekers of this sort find eventually that they fear death less and find life more deeply satisfying.

This book's title comes from Edith Sitwell's poem 'Eurydice':

Love is not changed by Death,
And nothing is lost and all in the end is harvest.

In one sense, of course, almost everything is lost when someone close to you dies – close love or affection, companionship, security and many other precious needs. And yet if 'nothing is lost' is taken to mean that no experience ultimately goes to waste if you make use of it, it is a profound truth, and it is one message this book tries to suggest. The sorrow, the anger and the guilt can often in time be turned to good account.

This book is the product of many suggestions for entries sent by Cruse members and workers all over Britain. It thus taps far greater experience and expertise than any I have myself.

Cruse Bereavement Care has many branches thoughout the United Kingdom. It aims to provide a multi-faceted response to the needs of bereaved people, but chiefly through counselling and befriending, through practical advice, and through social groups for those who need them. There is national membership for those who live where there is no branch yet. Cruse tries to provide some shelter through a very unhappy time, and an opportunity to take stock before moving on into a different sort of life.

My thanks go first to Hugh Rambaut, my father, for giving me an anthology at an early age (starting a lifelong addiction to them), and for transmitting the bottomless delight and solace of poetry. It was especially a saver of sanity for him in the trenches in France. Thank you also to my brother Richard, whose death led me up many blind alleys, but some of whose ideas I am catching up with now.

From every part of Cruse I have had assistance and support, so my thanks go to Colin Murray Parkes and the Council, Derek Nuttall, the staff of Cruse House, and the many members and workers who have sent suggestions. Warm thanks are also due to the many authors, executors and publishers who have generously given us permission to use copyright poems or prose extracts. I should also like to express my thanks to Enid Fennemore, who did the cover drawing, Dame Diana Reader Harris, Rachel Nugee, Metropolitan Anthony of Sourozh, Ronald Hamilton, and a host of other friends and colleagues; also Austin Whitaker (my Latin translator and father-in-law) and Antony Whitaker (my French translator and husband).

AGNES WHITAKER

1

We do have to grieve

. . . the heartbreak in the heart of things

W. W. GIBSON

In this section you will recognize many of the tumultuous feelings that come in the first weeks.

After eerie, non-feeling numbness comes a constant yearning, and there are sharp, aching pangs of grief.

There is the wish to honour and to idealize the person who has gone.

There is a sense of amputation, and a void that shows itself in every detail of life, especially the chair, the table-setting and the bed.

There are 'if onlys', the feeling that the world has gone upside-down, and a determination never to forget.

There can be a rage and bitterness you never expected, and a strong feeling of guilt, both of which sour the purer aspects of your grief.

There are tentative efforts to find meaning, and perhaps a longing to hide yourself away.

There is some cynicism, and there are isolated points of hope.

There is dreadful turmoil of mind, and quiet appreciation.

There is the feeling that you no longer want to live beyond tomorrow.

There is also the firm determination that the grief shall itself be a tribute.

Western Wind

Western wind, when wilt thou blow,
The small rain down can rain?
Christ, if my love were in my arms
And I in my bed again!

ANON *c.* 1500

From **Remembrance of Things Past**

People do not die for us immediately, but remain bathed in a sort
of *aura* of life which bears no relation to true immortality but
through which they continue to occupy our thoughts as when they
were alive. It is as though they were travelling abroad.

MARCEL PROUST

Disposing of Ashes

A gray day in June, as cold as charity,
The full-leaved trees sinister in heavy green,
The undertaker wearing his winter coat.
Our cold lies inside us like a cube of ice
Unmelting in the core of our being,
Untouched by succeeding summers,
For June will always be cold now,
However bright the sun, however fragmented
The light and shade, the over-blown rose,
The tall grasses seeding in a recession,
The tar bubbling on the hot road-ways.
Death stamps its mark on a month
And a year. Never will Jubilee tat
Be a joke any more. Sodden bunting
Hangs in the rain, swags and crowns
Disintegrate. Only the plastic flags
Survive, flapping disconsolately on fences
And front doors. It has been a wet week,
The street parties were a wash-out,
The public junketing an offence against
Private grief. Even Ditchling Beacon
Looks menacing, and the ashes not soft
As in imagination, but like pellets
Almost. We dump them among the rabbit
Droppings, and run through the mud
And drizzle, back to nothing
Where something was before,
Leaving our royal one soaking
Into the soft downland grass
Faceless to the sky.

ELIZABETH BARTLETT

It is arguable whether we write more or fewer personal letters to each other than we did fifty years ago. Certainly we send more greetings cards for family occasions, where in the past a letter might have been written. Interestingly, though, condolence letters are an exception to this trend. Many of us still try to send a condolence letter of sorts, though we all find them extremely hard to write. It is hard to settle down to write one, hard to find the appropriate words, hard to be sure they will strike the right note. Perhaps we feel we owe a letter to the memory of the person who has gone, and a card will not do. Cards do not record the unique qualities of the dead person, or the memories of treasured contacts with that person.

What do we want to say in a condolence letter? We want to acknowledge the immensity of the loss. So long as this is conveyed, it does not matter too much what the words are. Shocked and numbed and deeply sad most newly bereaved people may be, but they can still appreciate the effort and emotion put into a condolence letter, however clumsily.

There are universal sentiments in the letter quoted below. Perhaps the special quality here is the great beauty of the language, the use of only the simplest words.

I break in upon you at a moment, when we least of all are permitted to disturb our friends, only to say, that you are daily and hourly present to my thoughts. If the worst be not yet past, you will neglect and pardon me; but if the last struggle be over, if the poor object of your long anxieties be no longer sensible of your kindness, or to her own sufferings, allow me (at least in idea, for what could I do, were I present, more than this?) to sit by you in silence, and pity from my heart not her, who is at rest, but you, who lost her. May He, who made us, the master of our pleasures and of our pains, preserve and support you! Adieu.

I have long understood how little you had to hope.

LETTER FROM THOMAS GRAY TO WILLIAM MASON, 28 MARCH 1767

Mason comments:
As this little billet (which I received at the Hot Wells at Bristol) then breathed, and still seems to breathe, the very voice of friends in its tenderest and most pathetic note, I cannot refrain from publishing it in this place. I opened it almost at the precise moment which would necessarily be the most affecting.

From **Rosencrantz and Guildenstern are Dead**

No, no. It's not like that. Death isn't romantic . . . death is not anything . . . death is . . . not. It's the absence of presence, nothing more . . . the endless time of never coming back . . . a gap you can't see, and when the wind blows through it, it makes no sound.

TOM STOPPARD

The word grief is generally used to describe an individual's psychological process of adjusting to a close personal loss. The word mourning is often kept for social or conventional expressions of grief, but some of the writers in this book use it in a wider sense. The subtitle of Lily Pincus's much valued book 'Death and the Family' is 'The Importance of Mourning'. The passage here shows how a close personal relationship, perhaps with a counsellor if there is no suitable friend or relative to listen, can replace, in a way, the support of traditional, formal mourning rituals.

Rituals express the collective unconscious of the culture, for which they perform a religious, social or therapeutic function. For our western society, with its emphasis on close personal relationships, different – more personal – forms of *rites de passage* are necessary. In their absence, an increasing number of counselling services, set up by both voluntary and statutory organizations, are offering help to the individual bereaved or to small groups of mourners . . .

The majority of mourners may not actually make use of therapeutic services. Nevertheless, it may help them to know that they can do so, just as physical symptoms sometimes disappear as soon as the patient knows that he can go to see a doctor.

LILY PINCUS

From **In Loving Memory: E. M. Butler**

'Goodbye' – the number of times each day one says it!
But the goodbyes that matter we seldom say,
Being elsewhere – preoccupied, on a visit,
Somehow off guard – when the dear friend slips away

Tactfully, for ever. And had we known him
So near departure, would we have shut our eyes
To the leaving look in his? Tried to detain him
On the doorstep with bouquets of goodbyes?

I think of one, so constant a life-enhancer
That I can hardly yet imagine her dead;
Who seems, in her Irish courtesy, to answer
Even now the farewell I left unsaid.

Remembering her threefold self – a scholar,
A white witch, a small girl, fused into one –
Though all the love they lit will never recall her,
I warm my heart still at her cordial sun.

CECIL DAY LEWIS

When someone dies, Maoris perform the tangihana *ceremony before burial. The family sits with the body and each person who arrives is expected to greet both the dead and the living. The ensuing ceremonies confirm the reality of the death, and mourners rehearse the good and bad qualities of the deceased. It is a little like an Irish country wake. Much necessary mourning is done.*

A tangi is a cry or call. So these modern passages, written from within both a Maori and a Christian heritage, represent a crying out for the lost partner, anguished at first, but gradually more tranquil.

The Invocation *Kua whetarangitia ratou.*

They have become bright stars in the heavens
They have joined the firmament of the living God
The saints who through our Saviour's death
Traverse the route beyond death, to vibrant life
The knowing, the loving, the ever-present truth
Of life greater than Death, here, and beyond present touching
For this we praise you our Almighty Redeemer.

The First Tangi: Vigil. I wrote my offering to try to make sense of those first days, the first *tangi.* I had to have real things to grasp. I thought of the beehive in the garden.

One deadly moment wrenched my soul away
For in my bedroom chill death lay
Vibrant outside flowers touched the swarming bees
Tear washed inside sobbed flowers of grief

Yet you grew in us dear green-fingered Anne
Love's fragrant flowers in Heaven's garden
Your beauty of Love in God and God in Love
Your caress the soul dull tares remove
Kua whetarangitia koe, Anne.
You are our shining star now, Anne.

God help me see Anne's meaning through the earthly things around me. Things which carry the meaning and message of your vibrant earth, and her continued meaning in it.

So we had you in your coffin to lie with us in the house, our lover, to talk to, to know beyond death. To meditate with. To have time in our vigil to come to terms with your new being.

Your return from the mortuary brought us peace. Your death is real, it's physical, it's not a nightmare. And it's obviously not the end. God bless you for bringing us your peace. His peace.

The Second Tangi: Responses. They wrote to me; sensing the urgent need to see Eternity through tears, to see God's purpose.

While I fail to understand so very much in life, of this I am sure, that a person one loves dearly becomes very close in death. In the emptiness and pain there grows a surety, a trust and a knowledge that is greater than the moments one experiences in daily contact. These moments become an ever-present depth which grows in one's awareness and the 'sting' of death becomes hard to pinpoint. My prayer is to Anne that through her death she will be closer to you all in whatever it is that creates our Oneness. God bless you all.

The Third Tangi: Eulogies. Bless the fifteen-year-old, your son's friend, who searched for himself, asked where he fits into this drama.

I went straight to the chapel and I prayed. I thought there is very few people like your late wife. Whenever I came round I was always sure to be greeted with a smile and once even kissed goodbye. But now God has called her away to be with Him which no such person could deserve more than her.

Atiana wrote a *tangi pouri* for her:

> *Kua taka he puti puti ki te wai*
> *Kua puaretia ki te ao, i tena ataahua*
> *Kua tere ki runga ki te tai pari e*
> *Kua kauheketia ki te moana.*

I added:

> *Ki to moana o tatou Atua.*

> A flower has fallen into the water
> Its petals spread wide to show their beauty to the world
> It is caught by the falling tide
> And carried to the ocean
> of our God.

The Last Tangi

> *Haere haere ki te rangimarie.*
> Farewell to the place of peace
> Be with us in your peace our lover.

REX BLOOMFIELD

There are not many hymns in this anthology. 'Abide with Me' probably stands out among hymns that give support to the bereaved. Together with 'O God, Our Help', it is embedded in our consciousness as a community, and many know the words of both hymns by heart.

'Lead, Kindly Light' has possibly suffered something of an eclipse in recent years, but surely the last two lines of the first verse are made for the early months of bereavement. There is often no wish or ability to look further ahead than tomorrow.

> Lead, kindly light, amid the encircling gloom,
>   Lead thou me on;
> The night is dark, and I am far from home;
>   Lead thou me on.
> Keep thou my feet; I do not ask to see
> The distant scene: one step enough for me.

> I was not ever thus, nor prayed that thou
>   Shouldst lead me on;
> I loved to choose and see my path; but now
>   Lead thou me on.
> I loved the garish day, and, spite of fears,
> Pride ruled my will: remember not past years.

So long thy power hath blest me, sure it still
            Will lead me on
O'er moor and fen, o'er crag and torrent, till
            The night is gone,
And with the morn those angel faces smile
Which I have loved long since, and lost awhile.

JOHN HENRY NEWMAN

All is not lost

There is no magical anaesthetic for the pain of grief . . . We cannot give to the bereaved the one thing they most want; we cannot call back Lazarus, or Bert or Harry from the dead. The bereaved know that. They know that 'There is nothing you can say.' And they have seen others turn away, embarrassed by their uselessness. But anyone who turns towards the widow and the widower and gives confidence that they do have something to offer at moments of utter despair helps to reassure them that all is not lost. Goodness is not gone from the world because one good person has died. Meaning has not gone from life because one who meant so much is no longer present. The loss of one trusted person need not undermine trust in all of those who remain.

COLIN MURRAY PARKES

This poem is taken from an unusual anthology, 'The Penguin Book of Oral Poetry', which covers traditional verse from thirteen different cultures, normally passed down in the spoken word. It is a free translation of a traditional elegy by the Gond peasants in central India.

The Depths of Sorrow

The depths of sorrow in tears have not been measured.
The mountains and the hills will pass away
Like flooded rivers and streams, tears may flow
But what your destiny has given you must accept.
Brother, were I a teardrop I would fall like flooded waters
For the deep limits of sorrow's tears are not yet found.

Tam Cari Capitis

That the world will never be quite – what a cliché –
the same again
Is what we only learn by the event
When a friend dies out on us and is not there
To share the periphery of a remembered scent

Or leave his thumb-print on a shared ideal:
Yet it is not at floodlit moments we miss him most,
Not intervolution of wind-rinsed plumage of oatfield
Nor curragh dancing off a primeval coast

Nor the full strings of passion; it is in killing
Time where he would have livened it, such as the
drop-by-drop
Of games like darts or chess, turning the faucet
On full at a threat to the queen or double top.

LOUIS MACNEICE

In personal experiences such as giving birth, fighting sickness, or overco-
ming sorrow, some people do not want to know the psychological details
of what is happening. Others do: they feel a strong need to study the
theory – it can take some of the fear away.

This urge to find out, to research, can itself be part of the work of grief.
The great thing about it is that it achieves some results, whereas when
you mull over and over the events around the death there can be no
resolution until you begin to accept the death itself. If you are trying to
find out what is happening to you when you are grieving, you do get
some answers. You have the assurance that it has happened to thousands
of others in a similar way, though you may have had no inkling of it
before. You are so much comforted to know you are not going mad. If
you have constant imaginings that you, too, are suffering a mortal illness,
then the illness is highly unlikely; the imaginings are so very common in
grief. It all begins to make sense.

Until recently there were very few books written for bereaved people
that went into much detail. There were either simpler, supportive books
for the bereaved, or more complex theoretical material for counsellors and
helpers. Judy Tatelbaum's book 'The Courage to Grieve' fills this gap
well. It is a handbook to assist you to make the grief itself a tribute, an
offering, to the person you have lost, as well as being a positive way
through to recovery. This extract is from the first page of that book.

The death of a dear one is the most profound of all sorrows. The grief that comes with such a loss is intense and multifaceted, affecting our emotions, our bodies, and our lives. Grief is preoccupying and depleting. Emotionally, grief is a mixture of raw feelings such as sorrow, anguish, anger, regret, longing, fear, and deprivation. Grief may be experienced physically as exhaustion, emptiness, tension, sleeplessness, or loss of appetite. Grief invades our daily lives in many sudden gaps and changes, like that empty place at the dinner table, or the sudden loss of affection and companionship, as well as in many new apprehensions, adjustments, and uncertainties. The loss of a dear one throws every aspect of our lives out of balance. The closer we were to the person who died, the more havoc the loss creates. Love does not die quickly. Hence to grieve is also 'to celebrate the depth of the union. Tears are then the jewels of remembrance, sad but glistening with the beauty of the past. So grief in its bitterness marks the end . . . but it also is praise to the one who is gone.'

JUDY TATELBAUM

From **Grief**

> Pull down the tokens. Close your eyes,
> Hide from the sun. At least the night
> Will keep the pain from other people's sight
> And you'll have the stars' cold light.

ELIZABETH JENNINGS

Different aspects of loss

A counsellor who worked with the bereaved used to ask them to list the losses that the death they were mourning had brought them, in order to help them to uncover some of the depth of their loss.

The list usually started with obvious practical losses or related to new roles which the widow or widower now had to take over: father or mother to the children, chief breadwinner or cook, handyman, painter and decorator, gardener, shopper, banker, motor mechanic, etc. The most urgent of these roles were those that the survivor felt least able to fill, or which by his incompetence within it had led to embarrassment or catastrophe.

A widow whose husband had always looked after the car did not know that its engine needed oil; a widowed father found shopping and packing up his children's lunches a very daunting daily chore; the widow of an accountant had never written a cheque and was at a loss how to pay her gas bill. Unaccustomed jobs, even if small, loom large to those under stress.

This is an area in which friends and neighbours can be very helpful and supportive.

Deeper feelings are involved in the loss of the relationship itself. Parents have lost a part of themselves as well as a guarantee of their own continuity. Children will have lost their closest bond, their protector and provider and with this, their sense of security. The widowed have lost the one with whom they shared their home and family, their social companion, their sexual partner, their confidant/e and comforter – a specially poignant loss at this time of distress.

Loss is the sad refrain of the bereaved. They are both loser and lost.

ELIZABETH COLLICK

On the Death of His Father

I look up and see/his curtains and bed:
I look down and examine/his table and mat.
The things are there/just as before.
But the man they belonged to/is not there.
His spirit suddenly/has taken flight
And left me behind/far away.
To whom shall I look/on whom rely?
My tears flow/in an endless stream.
'Yu, yu'/cry the wandering deer
As they carry fodder/to their young in the wood.
Flap, flap/fly the birds
As they carry their little ones/back to the nest.
I alone/am desolate
Dreading the days/of our long parting:
My grieving heart's/settled pain
No one else/can understand.
There is a saying/among people
'Sorrow makes us/grow old.'
Alas, alas/for my white hairs!

All too early/they have come!
Long wailing,/long sighing
My thoughts are fixed on my sage parent.
They say the good/live long:
Then why was *he*/not spared?

TRANS. FROM THE CHINESE BY ARTHUR WALEY

From Gitanjali

If it is not my portion to meet thee in this my life
then let me ever feel that I have missed thy sight—let
me not forget for a moment, let me carry the pangs of
this sorrow in my dreams and in my wakeful hours.

As my days pass in the crowded market of this world
and my hands grow full with the daily profits, let me
ever feel that I have gained nothing—let me not forget
for a moment, let me carry the pangs of this sorrow in
my dreams and in my wakeful hours.

When I sit by the roadside, tired and panting, when
I spread my bed low in the dust, let me ever feel that
the long journey is still before me—let me not forget
for a moment, let me carry the pangs of this sorrow in
my dreams and in my wakeful hours.

When my rooms have been decked out and the flutes
sound and the laughter there is loud, let me ever feel
that I have not invited thee to my house—let me not
forget for a moment, let me carry the pangs of this
sorrow in my dreams and in my wakeful hours.

RABINDRANATH TAGORE

*Susan Wallbank is a Cruse counsellor. She has had several poems
published.*

Death makes philosophers of us all
the prospect of it in reality
disturbs time itself
lifelong patterns fall from us
as withered leaves lay bare the trees
in winter
and did we really yesterday believe
in mortgages and birthdays

in homes and holidays next year
in such blind innocence.
Philosophers are mad
or must become so
when face to face
with such great sadness.

SUSAN WALLBANK

After the death of a lifelong companion

Don't think I am unhappy and alone . . . I am in a new country
and she is the compass I travel by . . .
 I was grateful to you for your letter after Valentine's death, for
you were the sole person who said that for pain and loneliness
there is no cure. I suppose people have not the moral stamina to
contemplate the idea of no cure, and to ease their uneasiness they
trot out the most astonishing placebos. I was assured I would find
consolation in writing, in gardening, in tortoises, in tapestry . . .
in keeping bees, in social service . . ., and many of these consolers
were people whom I had previously found quite rational. Your
only runner-up was Reynolds Stone's wife, who said whisky . . .
But when one has had one's head cut off . . .

SYLVIA TOWNSEND WARNER

Aridity

My heart is empty. All the fountains that should run
With longing, are in me
Dried up. In all my countryside there is not one
That drips to find the sea.
I have no care for anything thy love can grant
Except the moment's vain
And hardly noticed filling of the moment's want
And to be free of pain.
Oh, thou that art unwearying, that dost neither sleep
Nor slumber, who didst take
All care for Lazarus in the careless tomb, oh keep
Watch for me while I wake.
If thou think for me what I cannot think, if thou
Desire for me what I

Cannot desire, my soul's interior Form, though now
Deep-buried, will not die,
– No more than the insensible dropp'd seed which grows
Through winter ripe for birth
Because, while it forgets, the heaven remembering throws
Sweet influence still on earth,
– Because the heaven, moved moth-like by thy beauty, goes
Still turning round the earth.

C. S. LEWIS

*The following extracts come from a sensitively written novel about
bereavement, 'Perfect Happiness' by Penelope Lively.*

. . . Happiness, of course, is forever bound to place, to the
physical world. We are never happy now, only then. Walking then
on a Dorset hill, wind lifting the hair, and a hand, suddenly, on
one's back . . . Sunlight sifting down through the apple tree in the
garden at Pulborough, lying like coins among the daisies of the
lawn. Happiness is out there, back there, in association with those
sights and sounds, and to retrieve it is to retrieve them also, to
bring them crowding into the dark bedroom at three in the
morning: mocking. Perfect happiness, past perfect, pluperfect.

Unhappiness, now so intimately known, is a very different
matter. Unhappiness is now, not then at all. Unhappiness is like
being in love: it occupies every moment of every day. It will not
be put aside and like love it isolates; grief is never contagious.

Loss clamped her every morning as she woke; it sat its grinding
weight on her and rode her, like the old man of the sea. It roared
in her ears when people talked to her so that frequently she did
not hear what they said. It interrupted her when she spoke, so that
she faltered in mid-sentence, lost track. A little less, now; remis-
sions came and went. The days stalked by, taking her with
them. . . .

During the early days and weeks of her solitude Frances had
come to realise that grief like illness is unstable; it ebbs and flows
in tides, it steals away to a distance and then comes roaring back,
it torments by deception. It plays games with time and with reality.
On some mornings she would wake and Steven's presence was so
distant and yet so reassuring that she thought herself purged; he
seemed both absent and present, she felt close to him and at the

same time freed, she thought that at last she was walking alone. And then, within hours she would be back once more in that dark trough: incredulous, raging, ground into her misery. Time, that should be linear, had become formless; mercurial and unreliable, it took her away from the moment of Steven's death and then flung her back beside it.

PENELOPE LIVELY

Sheila Hancock sent us this poem to put in the anthology, and in her accompanying letter she describes it as 'deeply felt and hopeful'. Sheila read it on the radio a few years ago, and it evoked a widespread response.

Grief

Deep sobs –
that start beneath my heart
and hold my body in a grip that hurts.
The lump that swells inside my throat
brings pain that tries to choke.
Then tears course down my cheeks –
I drop my head in my so empty hands
abandoning myself to deep dark grief
and know that with the passing time
will come relief.
That though the pain may stay
There soon will come a day
When I can say her name and be at peace.

NORAH LENEY

From **Gitanjali**

In desperate hope I go and search for her in all the corners of my room: I find her not.

My house is small and what once has gone from it can never be regained.

But infinite is thy mansion, my Lord, and seeking her I have come to thy door.

I stand under the golden canopy of thine evening sky and I lift my eager eyes to thy face.

I have come to the brink of eternity from which
nothing can vanish – no hope, no happiness, no vision
of a face seen through tears.

Oh, dip my emptied life into that ocean, plunge it
into the deepest fullness. Let me for once feel that lost
sweet touch in the allness of the universe.

RABINDRANATH TAGORE

*For generations, many have found the psalms a wonderful storehouse of
support at the worst times.*

*Some of the psalms express the Old Testament notions of a dreadful
fate befalling one's enemies, and occasionally the psalmist even proposes
a deal with God: if I am dutiful, respect you, etc., will you do some dirty
work for me, and make sure my enemies are beaten down?*

*In between all that, however, one keeps finding three verses here, four
there, and occasionally whole psalms, filled with the most loving, tender
and understanding thoughts.*

One example is given here.

Save me, O God: for the waters are come in, even unto my soul.

I stick fast in the deep mire, where no ground is: I am come
into deep waters, so that the floods run over me.

I am weary of crying; my throat is dry: my sight faileth me for
waiting so long upon my God . . .

Take me out of the mire, that I sink not: O let me be delivered
from them that hate me, and out of the deep waters.

Let not the water-flood drown me, neither let the deep swallow
me up: and let not the pit shut her mouth upon me.

Hear me, O Lord, for thy loving-kindness is comfortable: turn
thee unto me according to the multitude of thy mercies.

PSALM 69:1–3, 15–17

By all accounts Emily Brontë never had a lover. It is thought that this passionate poem was written after the death of her brother Branwell, who had caused the family so much worry.

Remembrance

Cold in the earth – and the deep snow piled above thee,
Far, far removed, cold in the dreary grave!
Have I forgot, my only Love, to love thee,
Severed at last by Time's all-severing wave? . . .

Cold in the earth – and fifteen wild Decembers,
From those brown hills have melted into spring:
Faithful indeed is the spirit that remembers
After such years of change and suffering!

Sweet Love of youth, forgive if I forget thee
While the world's tide is bearing me along;
Other desires and other hopes beset me,
Hopes which obscure, but cannot do thee wrong!

No later light has lightened up my heaven;
No second morn has ever shone for me:
All my life's bliss from thy dear life was given,
All my life's bliss is in the grave with thee.

But, when the days of golden dreams had perished,
And even Despair was powerless to destroy,
Then did I learn how existence could be cherished,
Strengthened, and fed without the aid of joy;

Then did I check the tears of useless passion,
Weaned my young soul from yearning after thine;
Sternly denied its burning wish to hasten
Down to that tomb already more than mine.

And, even yet, I dare not let it languish,
Dare not indulge in Memory's rapturous pain;
Once drinking deep of that divinest anguish,
How could I seek the empty world again?

EMILY BRONTË

John Bowlby and his wife selected these extracts from Tennyson's 'In Memoriam', and urged that we include them. Their accompanying letter said:

'We were both put off reading it by its extreme length, and our elders' contemptuous view of it – "just a Victorian wallow in death!" It burst on our consciousness about a year ago.

'It took Tennyson seventeen years to write – Hallam died in 1833, and the poem was published (anon) in 1850. It isn't chronological, but consists of a number of different ways people can express their agonized grief. We suppose it must be by far the greatest poem on loss ever written. We had great difficulty in finding a part of it offering any comfort at all, but in the end we did. The whole poem is written in the same haunting verse-form, which links it.

'As far as consolation is concerned, all one can say is that bereaved people can read Tennyson's marvellous poetry and know he has been there himself and recognizes the landscape of bereavement and loss.'

From **In Memoriam**

This truth came borne with bier and pall,
I felt it, when I sorrowed most.
'Tis better to have loved and lost
Than never to have loved at all –

O true in word, and tried in deed,
Demanding, so to bring relief
To this which is our common grief,
What kind of life is that I lead;

And whether trust in things above
Be dimmed of sorrow, or sustained;
And whether love for him have drained
My capabilities of love. . . .

But I remained, whose hopes were dim,
Whose life, whose thoughts were little worth,
To wander on a darkened earth,
Where all things round me breathed of him. . . .

Yet more could better know than I,
How much of art at human hands
The sense of human will demands
By which we dare to live or die.

Whatever way my days decline,
I felt, and feel, though left alone,
His being working in mine own,
The footsteps of his life in mine; . . .

And so my passion hath not swerved
To works of weakness, but I find
An image comforting the mind,
And in my grief a strength reserved.

                                        ALFRED, LORD TENNYSON

Lament

We who are left, how shall we look again
Happily on the sun or feel the rain,
Without remembering how they who went
Ungrudgingly, and spent
Their all for us, loved too the sun and rain?

A bird among the rain-wet lilac sings –
But we, how shall we turn to little things,
And listen to the birds and winds and streams
Made holy by their dreams,
Nor feel the heart-break in the heart of things?

                                        W. W. GIBSON

In Memory of My Mother

You will have the road gate open, the front door ajar
The kettle boiling and a table set
By the window looking out at the sycamores –
And your loving heart lying in wait

For me coming up among the poplar trees.
You'll know my breathing and my walk
And it will be a summer evening on those roads
Lonely with leaves of thought.

We will be choked with the grief of things growing,
The silence of dark-green air
Life too rich – the nettles, docks and thistles
All answering the prodigal's prayer.

You will know I am coming though I send no word
For you were lover who could tell
A man's thoughts – my thoughts – though I hid them –
Through you I knew Woman and did not fear her spell.

                                    PATRICK KAVANAGH

*Brenda Lismer is a Cruse member who wrote two poems for possible
inclusion in the 'Cruse Chronicle', the newsletter which Cruse sends
each month to widowed members. Both were published, and both have
been appreciated and cherished by many readers. The second poem appears
on page 137.*

Sharing

Autumn was our time of year
Working together in the old walled garden
Not speaking so much as sharing
The silence and September warmth
The gentleness of slow decay
At summer's passing.

I was the debris man clearing the way
You turned the dark earth with your spade
Slow and steady knowing your pace
Turned tramp in your awful gardening clothes
Which somehow became dear.

I miss your patient figure
As I harvest alone
Miss the shared silence
And the coming together at day's end.

                                    BRENDA LISMER

2

The landscape of bereavement and loss

In troubled Water you can scarce see your Face, or see it very little, till the Water be quiet and stand still. So in troubled times you can see little Truth; when times are quiet and settled, Truth appears.

JOHN SELDEN

There are some general patterns of grief, but in the details each person is unique, as befits human beings.

Shock, numbness and disbelief will normally be greater, and last longer, when the death was sudden and unexpected, than when there was a long illness – though there can be some disbelief even after many months of nursing someone who gradually became sicker. The anguish of intense pangs of grief and sheer yearning, with the release of weeping, may last weeks for some people, but unremittingly for months and even years for others. Tremendous anger, rage and bitterness may be part of the scene in the early weeks, directed against doctors or a casualty department, the hospital, the dead person, against God or providence. Those who find themselves on the receiving end of this anger must make enormous allowances for the situation and try not to take it on board personally.

Feelings of self-reproach may arise, however unwarranted. You may find causes for self-reproach in relationships in the past; there seems to be no way, now, of resolving conflicts that were never resolved earlier, and no opportunity to make amends for any ill-considered, hurtful remarks you made. You may tend to blame yourself in the circumstances of the death – in fact, almost everyone does. Your hasty decisions at moments of shock and panic were most probably the best in the circumstances, but you often doubt it now. You can feel guilty about some of the resentments and critical thoughts about the dead person that are emerging now, and about the anger that may be welling up, some of it directed against the very person you are grieving for. It is quite common, and very understandable, for someone who is grieving to rage against the very person they have lost – for going away and leaving them. In the particularly hard circumstances *of bereavement after suicide, when feelings of self-reproach can be almost unbearable, we might try to separate the unacceptable* method *of death from everything else about that person's life and the fact of the death. In all circumstances, both anger and self-reproach can take you back again and again, mulling over significant memories in a seemingly fruitless and negative way. And yet it is not just negative; the continual yearning, even in these apparently contrary ways, is grief work being done.*

Among the turbulent whirlpools of emotions that grief precipitates, one also finds the opposite of anger and guilt – a loss of aggressiveness and courage, an apathy, and feelings of defeatism, despair and depression. Very often these more passive phenomena are a slightly later development, bringing their own particular form of misery at a time when the sharpest pangs of sadness begin to be less frequent, less intense. Eventually one can reach a nadir, an all-time low, when life seems to have little real meaning any more, and you only live from day to day. You see no way in which this can ever change. How can life have any real meaning now? How can you find any deep security or happiness ever again?

If only one could hurry through all these dreadful feelings – by denying them, by being 'busy' or organized. But that is worse. If the feelings are there, they must come out, like the pus in a wound. And much time is needed, for all the sorrow to be expended, all the healing to be done.

So how can one get through? How can anyone else help? Really close relatives and friends, or befriending counsellors, can be of the greatest help – just sharing the feelings, letting them be aired, if necessary many times.

If you feel that you are going backwards – back to more frequent pangs of grief, back to deep bitterness or searing self-reproach – then it is surely not for long. It is as if these aspects of grief must have a final go at you before they disappear. They will, almost entirely, in the end.

From **Ross**

I will not insult you by trying to tell you that one day you will forget. I know as well as you that you will not. But, at least, in time you will not remember as fiercely as you do now – and I pray that that time may be soon.

TERENCE RATTIGAN

From **Macbeth**

> Give sorrow words. The grief that does not speak
> Whispers the o'erfraught heart, and bids it break.

WILLIAM SHAKESPEARE

Talking of Death

My friend was dead. A simple sentence ended
With one black stop, like this: My friend was dead.
I had no notion that I had depended
So much on fires he lit, on that good bread
He always had to offer if I came
Hungry and cold to his inviting room.
Absurdly, I believed that he was lame
Until I started limping from his tomb.
My sorrow was the swollen, prickly kind,
Not handsome mourning smartly cut and pressed:
An actual grief, I swear. Therefore to find
Myself engaged upon a shameful quest
For anyone who'd known him, but who thought
That he was still alive, was something strange,
Something disquieting; for what I sought
Was power and presence beyond my usual range.
For once, my audience listened, welcomed me,
Avid for every syllable that spoke
Of woven fear and grieving. Nervously
They eyed my black, ambassadorial cloak.
Their faces greyed; my friend's death died, and they
Saw theirs walk in alive. I felt quite well –
Being Death's man – until they went away,
And I was left with no one else to tell.

VERNON SCANNELL

Fears of madness

The bereaved have lost someone infinitely significant for whom
there is no substitute. They have this urgent restless need to search
and to find; their searching is natural in their loss, but it cannot
succeed because the object they seek is a living person. The one

they so desperately need to find, for whom they must search and
search, is the one they know and love. They seek the living: their
search is vain because the one they love is no longer alive. . . .

To find oneself behaving unusually, irrationally, yet restless and
frustrated if one tries to stop; not to know why one is doing what
it seems one must do; to feel ashamed and foolish and unable to
explain; to find no comfort or satisfaction from one's restless activity; this is a bewildering, frightening experience in an already
distressing situation. 'Am I going mad?' is the question so often
asked, and probably even more often feared and ashamedly
unasked.

When something of this concept of loss-and-search is understood, mourners are often relieved and comforted to discover that
behaviour which seemed inexplicable, uncontrollable, senseless and
disturbing, is a normal universal bereavement experience. This will
not ease the urgent need to search, but it goes some way towards
relieving the bewilderment and distress. It may make, too, for
more compassionate understanding from those around if they are
able to recognize something of what lies behind this compulsive
restlessness.

ELIZABETH COLLICK

Ox-Eye Daisies, Loweswater, One June Day

White, whiter than shroud fresh laundered,
Wide petals wreathe their golden stare –
Eyes of the day blind to the night's dark hours
One by one I break their dry, ribbed stems
Just as, last year, we plucked their kin together
As life itself so suddenly is plucked
And I severed from its roots while yet in flower;
Everything looks so *terribly* the same –
Even my face, shock-wiped as clear of woe
As the lake's glass is cleared of last night's storm.
The same sun brightens, falsely reassures
That nothing has changed, and the world goes on
Even as I pick these flowers to fill the house
For that pitiless, empty day not dwelt upon;
Half of me gropes through an unlighted dream
Seeking an exit; this was your favourite shore –
This is your favourite shore – or do you watch me now

From a more distant strand? Still I go on
Harvesting daisies, leaves from the ledges, bracken,
Not just to make the house beautiful for you
But that, for now, what else is there to do?

SALLY THOMPSON

Healthy and unhealthy grieving

Healthy grief, dramatic and even traumatic as it may be, is a three-
stage process. First, it is fully experiencing and expressing all the
emotions and reactions to the loss. Second, it is completing and
letting go of your attachment both to the deceased and to sorrow.
Third, it is recovering and reinvesting anew in one's own life.
Missing any of the steps in the grieving process may result in
unhealthy or unsuccessful grief. Because these stages may take
many months, unsuccessful grief may not show up until long after
the loss. However, when even unsuccessful grief becomes evident,
it can be explored and successfully resolved. Unsuccessful grief is
usually reversible.

For us to complete every step of the grieving process requires
awareness, courage, openness, self-support, and support from
others. Because of the complexity of this process, many of us do
not fully complete each necessary step. That is why unsuccessful
or unhealthy grief is common. Further complicating our completion of the grieving process is the fact that our responses to loss
are often automatic or unconscious, so that we may be unaware
of what we are going through.

Since the grieving process is mostly learned, few of us experience
healthy grief without first using more unsuitable means for coping
with our pain and sorrow . . .

Unsuccessful grief is also the result of the misguided ideas of
courage in our society. For example, courage is often seen as a
capacity to be silent when in pain, to control tears at all costs, to
function regardless of the depths of turmoil inside us, and to handle
our wounds and sorrows privately and independently. Few of us
are so superhuman. When we try to act according to these ideals,
we usually deny our pain and never learn to cope with it. Since
pain unexpressed does not dissolve spontaneously, we may suffer
severe consequences from pretending to be superhuman . . .

It takes enormous courage to face pain directly and honestly, to
sit in the midst of such uncomfortable feelings and reactions until

we have expressed them and finished with them. It takes courage
to be willing to experience fully the pain and anguish of grief and
to face feelings at the time they occur rather than postponing the
encounter.

JUDY TATELBAUM

From Seventeen Old Poems

The dead are gone and with them we cannot converse.
The living are here and ought to have our love.
Leaving the city-gate I look ahead
And see before me only mounds and tombs.
The old graves are ploughed up into fields,
The pines and cypresses are hewn for timber.
In the white aspens sad winds sing;
Their long murmuring kills my heart with grief.
I want to go home, to ride to my village gate.
I want to go back, but there's no road back.

TRANS. FROM THE CHINESE BY ARTHUR WALEY

Musée des Beaux Arts

About suffering they were never wrong,
The Old Masters: how well they understood
Its human position; how it takes place
While someone else is eating or opening a window or just
    walking dully along;
How, when the aged are reverently, passionately waiting
For the miraculous birth, there always must be
Children who did not specially want it to happen, skating
On a pond at the edge of the wood:
They never forgot
That even the dreadful martyrdom must run its course
Anyhow in a corner, some untidy spot
Where the dogs go on with their doggy
    life and the torturer's horse
Scratches its innocent behind on a tree.

In Breughel's *Icarus*, for instance: how everything turns away
Quite leisurely from the disaster; the ploughman may
Have heard the splash, the forsaken cry,
But for him it was not an important failure; the sun shone
As it had to on the white legs disappearing into the green
Water; and the expensive delicate ship that must have seen
Something amazing, a boy falling out of the sky,
Had somewhere to get to and sailed calmly on.

W. H. AUDEN

*Surely G. M. Hopkins's disjointed and seemingly incoherent style exactly
matches the things he is saying in this poem. He plumbs the very depths.*
   *You may be at that place yourself. Perhaps you feel more anguished
yearning than you did a month or two ago, and your aloneness is beginning
to show itself in its full force. Are there lower depths still? Is there no
way out?*
   *There is, there really is, but it comes inch by inch, in tiny steps, and
some of those backwards. One day soon you will find you do not suffer
any of these dreadful pangs of grief for several hours at a time. The next
few days may be as bad as ever, but then there is another lighter, freer
day. Something hopeful is happening at last. Watch for the smallest signs,
and hang on to the hope and promise of the good days.*

No Worst, There is None

No worst, there is none. Pitched past pitch of grief,
More pangs will, schooled at forepangs, wilder wring.
Comforter, where, where is your comforting?
Mary, mother of us, where is your relief?
My cries heave, herds-long; huddle in a main, a chief
Woe, world-sorrow; on an age-old anvil wince and sigh –
Then lull, then leave off. Fury had shrieked 'No ling-
ering! Let me be fell: force I must be brief.'

O the mind, mind has mountains; cliffs of fall
Frightful, sheer, no-man-fathomed. Hold them cheap
May who ne'er hung there. Nor does long our small
Durance deal with that steep or deep. Here! creep,
Wretch, under a comfort serves in a whirlwind: all
Life death does end and each day dies with sleep.

GERARD MANLEY HOPKINS

As a book of reflections on grief, by someone bereaved, C. S. Lewis's 'A Grief Observed' probably stands quite alone for its detailed insight and beautifully expressed analysis of feelings as they appear. It is not soothing reading: some find its stark comments lay bare too many raw feelings. At one point, for instance, he says: 'What pitiable cant to say "She will live for ever in my memory". Live? That is exactly what she won't do.'

Yet there are many immensely helpful insights if you can press on with the book, either straight away, or after laying it down for a month or two.

No one ever told me that grief felt so like fear. I am not afraid, but the sensation is like being afraid. The same fluttering in the stomach, the same restlessness, the yawning. I keep on swallowing.

At other times it feels like being mildly drunk, or concussed. There is a sort of invisible blanket between the world and me. I find it hard to take in what anyone says. Or perhaps, hard to want to take it in. It is so uninteresting. Yet I want the others to be about me. I dread the moments when the house is empty. If only they would talk to one another and not to me . . .

And grief still feels like fear. Perhaps, more strictly, like suspense. Or like waiting; just hanging about waiting for something to happen. It gives life a permanently provisional feeling. It doesn't seem worth starting anything. I can't settle down. I yawn, I fidget, I smoke too much. Up till this I always had too little time. Now there is nothing but time. Almost pure time, empty successiveness . . .

I think I am beginning to understand why grief feels like suspense. It comes from the frustration of so many impulses that had become habitual. Thought after thought, feeling after feeling, action after action, had H. for their object. Now their target is gone. I keep on through habit fitting an arrow to the string; then I remember and have to lay the bow down. So many roads lead thought to H. I set out on one of them. But now there's an impassable frontier-post across it. So many roads once; now so many *culs de sac*. . . .

Tonight all the hells of young grief have opened again; the mad words, the bitter resentment, the fluttering in the stomach, the nightmare unreality, the wallowed-in tears. For in grief nothing 'stays put'. One keeps on emerging from a phase, but it always recurs. Round and round. Everything repeats. Am I going in circles, or dare I hope I am on a spiral?

But if a spiral, am I going up or down it? . . .

Sorrow, however, turns out to be not a state but a process. It needs not a map but a history, and if I don't stop writing that history at some quite arbitrary point, there's no reason why I should ever stop. There is something new to be chronicled every day. Grief is like a long valley, a winding valley where any bend may reveal a totally new landscape. As I've already noted, not every bend does. Sometimes the surprise is the opposite one; you are presented with exactly the same sort of country you thought you had left behind miles ago. That is when you wonder whether the valley isn't a circular trench. But it isn't. There are partial recurrences, but the sequence doesn't repeat.

C. S. LEWIS

From **Words about Grief**

Time does not heal,
It makes a half-stitched scar
That can be broken and you feel
Grief as total as in its first hour.

ELIZABETH JENNINGS

My father's copy of W. E. Henley's poems bears the inscription 'From F. E. H., 23 August 1940'. That date was significant to anyone living in Britain then, with the imminent threat of a German invasion. F. E. H. was a colleague at work, and their office was in Hibernia Chambers, a fine early-Victorian building which still stands, on the south approaches to London Bridge; so they must have been frighteningly exposed to the blitz.

Perhaps this poem has been half-forgotten. It is wonderfully helpful in all kinds of harrowing situations, not only bereavement. You can mutter it to yourself defiantly.

Out of the night that covers me,
  Black as the pit from pole to pole
I thank whatever gods may be
  For my unconquerable soul.

In the fell clutch of circumstance
  I have not winced nor cried aloud.
Under the bludgeonings of chance
  My head is bloody, but unbowed.

Beyond this place of wrath and tears
  Looms but the Horror of the shade,
And yet the menace of the years
  Finds and shall find me unafraid.

It matters not how strait the gate,
  How charged with punishments the scroll,
I am the master of my fate:
  I am the captain of my soul.

                                    W. E. HENLEY

Sir Francis Meynell was the son of Alice Meynell, and godson of Francis Thompson. An artist in the field of print, and a publisher, he was also a fine poet.

Substitute

Warm from his arms, his broken
Good-bye, you clung to me.
These were your words, soft spoken:
'Read me some poetry'.

Then I, his voice supplying,
The shadow of his shade,
Read, where we two were lying,
The words he might have read.

We offered for love's aiding
Measure and over-press:
My monstrous masquerading,
Your little loneliness.

                    SIR FRANCIS MEYNELL

Cecil Day Lewis, in an anthology, called this poem by Dylan Thomas 'a kind of squaring up to death'. As well as recalling, and trying to find reconciliation with, the memory of those who rebelled against dying, this poem's power can surely also be harnessed in our anger about the death. Why should someone be allowed to disappear gently, quietly, without a feeling of outrage? And yet even the poet acknowledges death as 'that good night'. You may not at first face it gently, but maybe you do not have to fight it for ever.

Do Not Go Gentle into that Good Night

Do not go gentle into that good night,
Old age should burn and rave at close of day;
Rage, rage against the dying of the light.

Though wise men at their end know dark is right.
Because their words have forked no lightning they
Do not go gentle into that good night.

Good men, the last wave by, crying how bright
Their frail deeds might have danced in a green bay,
Rage, rage against the dying of the light.

Wild men who caught and sang the sun in flight,
And learn, too late, they grieved it on its way,
Do not go gentle into that good night.

Grave men, near death, who see with blinding sight
Blind eyes could blaze like meteors and be gay,
Rage, rage against the dying of the light.

And you, my father, there on the sad height,
Curse, bless, me now with your fierce tears, I pray.
Do not go gentle into that good night.
Rage, rage against the dying of the light.

DYLAN THOMAS

We need to have the patterns of grief charted

One of the things I have learned through all this is that we who
have words can articulate grief for those who have not, and that
to have grief spelt out, its pattern charted, is something we all
obscurely need . . .

The thing to remember about bereavement is that one does what
one must, and no one can imagine what this may be before it
happens. I, who knew very well that the likelihood was that I
would be a widow someday, had felt quite sure that if and when
it happened I would run to my good friend Helen. In the event, I
found that nothing would have dragged me away from the home
which was, so to speak, the crown of our thirty years of happy
life together. Other widows run away from their home in horror;
a few never go back. But our dear house and garden, K's presence
there, the friendship of my neighbours, proved the only strength

I had. Unlike many bereaved women I was not afraid to go to bed alone at night – I had done that for most of the years of our marriage. And I did not really think out whether I *had* to go to work. That was the pattern of my life and it did not occur to me to wonder whether it should be changed. There were the letters to answer, two or three hundred of them. For a writing woman this may have been cathartic. For others it might have been an impossible burden, but I think that there are very few people who are not helped a little by having the 'condolence' letters. 'They are so hard to write,' people say. 'Whatever can one say?' It doesn't matter much what, though it is best if one can say something in praise of the person who has died. The comfort lies in the fact that the pile of letters indicates your grief has some importance, however brief. You may need to go back to them again and again later when everyone else seems to have forgotten and you yourself are more afraid of forgetting than of remembering . . .

Grief is an illness of the psyche. To formalize opportunities for its release, for weeping, wailing, yelling at fate is unlikely to help. Tears don't come to order and if they did, how could they bring relief? Rage creeps up on you unawares too. I was coming back from London and as I walked along a crowded compartment and saw people laughing and talking and reading and sleeping something in my mind went briefly out of gear. Their normality was hideous to me. I was in hostile country, an enemy alien. Fortunately two friends were waiting for me at the end of my journey. The mental processes slipped back into gear. It does not happen so quickly for everyone. I used to say for myself that like Katherine Mansfield's poor 'Ma Parker' I had no private place to cry. It wasn't true, because I had a whole empty house to cry in – but so often the need for tears came when I was at work, when it could not be satisfied. The body's protest at this rigid self-discipline was the quite terrifying exhaustion that came over me at times, so that I could barely lift my hand from the arm of a chair. As with many another woman, the sense of loss sometimes manifested itself in a searing physical pain, somewhere in the guts. It might have gone more easily for me if I had not slammed the door as tightly as I could on recollection of what had happened – I came to think later that I had slammed it against K as well as against anguish – but at the time there was no question of choice. In grief we do as we must . . .

It was a little later that it came to me that there was no one I could talk to as of right. When you are suddenly bereft of your 'speech-friend' (as William Morris called it) you fear that by engaging in conversation with anyone else you are asking a favour. Social assurance is more precarious than we think, for it rests on the assumption that by and large it is mutually agreeable. Gauche adolescents find it impossible to believe that anyone could actually enjoy talking to them; so do people whose inner security has collapsed, through bereavement, divorce, desertion, disgrace, being made redundant or any other reason. I began to have some insight into loneliness, the creeping paralysis of the social responses . . .

I was hollow inside. I was less than half a person. Behind the carefully maintained façade there was nothing, or at least nothing that really mattered. I must try to explain about this phase of bereavement because only those who have been through it know about it, and it is, I am certain, about three months after the death, when many of us appear to be doing quite nicely, that the collapse of the will to live occurs. It is then that widows, and widowers too, especially if they have no dependent children, need to be taken into the care of their friends. What needs to be done is just to keep them ticking over; to ask them on little visits, give them little jobs to do, nothing very much, nothing very demanding, just small things to fill in the emptiness of the personality as well as of the days. At this stage, Death is the friend, Life is the enemy. It seemed to me at this time that being alive was just a habit, and a habit that had now become very disagreeable. Now I had been jolted out of the normal view that it is obviously better to be alive than dead, it seemed a ludicrous proposition. What was so wonderful about being alive? Sixty years of life had habituated me to eating at certain times, washing, dressing, going to work, doing this and that – but *what for?* Why spend another ten or twenty years doing all these things just for the sake of being alive? There were, it is true, fleeting moments of pleasure but there was nothing, *nothing*, that made the future look anything but a dreary, meaningless trudge. The concept of life as a duty, in the abstract, struck me as monstrous. . . .

Perhaps the discovery that mourning does not preclude belly-aching laughter is a turning-point. It takes a long while for the bereaved to experience conscious happiness; much longer to admit to being happy, for that seems an intolerable disloyalty. Yet the return to normality has to be at the cost of the recession of the lost one. One may say, and often does, that the bloodiest anguish is better than forgetting, but the anguish slowly, and by no means steadily, recedes too . . .

That is how it is with the crippling effect of grief. Life creeps in unawares to restore the mutilated personality. For weeks I was a non-person, for many, many months a half-person and now I have to admit – reluctantly, because it was better to be part of a dual entity – that I am at least as much a whole person as many people who have never been chopped in half. I never consciously sought to create 'a life of my own', nor indeed actively hoped for or wanted it. It just happened, gradually, by doing what I had to do, by very determinedly filling up all the hours so that I seldom mouldered away on my own, by responding civilly, even if not with enthusiasm, to whatever invitations or stimuli came my way – and by quite savagely rejecting the idea that the widow should be a lifelong object of pity or, indeed, is more to be pitied than many other people who have suffered cruel loss or rejection, or who have never enjoyed the fullness of life. Several times I explored this thought in my *Guardian* writings and once with a hard irony that, to my sorrow, caused acute pain to women whose bereavement, whose wounds, were more raw than mine. It was about The Club, that sisterhood for widows which can be such a tender support and such a dangerous encouragement to trying to live in the past. Should I have written it, should it have been published? I don't know. I only know that if the mutilated personality is to survive it cannot be by trying to keep the Other alive, by emotional self-indulgence; it can only be by letting the habit of living take over until one can respond again to what life has to offer. As it gradually took over for me.

MARY STOTT

Grief

I tell you hopeless grief is passionless;
That only men incredulous of despair,
Half-taught in anguish, through the midnight air
Beat upward to God's throne in loud access
Of shrieking and reproach. Full desertness
In souls, as countries, lieth silent-bare
Under the blanching, vertical eye-glare
Of the absolute Heavens. Deep-hearted man, express
Grief for thy Dead in silence like to death–

Most like a monumental statue set
In everlasting watch and moveless woe
Till itself crumble to the dust beneath.
Touch it; the marble eyelids are not wet;
If it could weep it could arise and go.

ELIZABETH BARRETT BROWNING

*Most books of comforting verse for the widowed assume that every marriage
has been happy, and that the ensuing grief is relatively pure. This is
wishful thinking, or not-thinking, for there can be anger and guilt after
the happiest of marriages has ended in death. And as for those many
whose marriages became unsatisfying, bitter or deeply unhappy, they are
simply not catered for. Yet each widowed person must find inner peace,
starting from whatever position they are in – whatever the marriage was
like.*

*Thomas Hardy is here looking back to days of early happiness. So this
poem is for those who have not had much married happiness in recent
years. The grief is not only for the death, but for the earlier loss of close
contact, the loss of mutual joy and delight. It is helpful and therapeutic
to go right back to the good days.*

After a Journey

Hereto I come to view a voiceless ghost;
    Whither, O whither will its whim now draw me?
Up the cliff, down, till I'm lonely, lost,
    And the unseen waters' ejaculations awe me.
Where you will next be there's no knowing,
    Facing round about me everywhere,
        With your nut-coloured hair,
And grey eyes, and rose-flush coming and going.

Yes: I have re-entered your olden haunts at last;
    Through the years, through the dead scenes I have tracked
        you;
What have you now found to say of our past –
    Scanned across the dark space wherein I have lacked you?
Summer gave us sweets, but autumn wrought division?
    Things were not lastly as firstly well
        With us twain, you tell?
But all's closed now, despite Time's derision.

I see what you are doing: you are leading me on
    To the spots we knew when we haunted here together,
The waterfall, above which the mist-bow shone
    At the then fair hour in the then fair weather,
And the cave just under, with a voice still so hollow
    That it seems to call out to me from forty years ago,
        When you were all aglow,
And not the thin ghost that I now frailly follow!

Ignorant of what there is flitting here to see,
    The waked birds preen and the seals flop lazily;
Soon you will have, Dear, to vanish from me,
    For the stars close their shutters and the dawn whitens hazily.
Trust me, I mind not, though Life lours,
    The bringing me here; nay, bring me here again!
        I am just the same as when
Our days were a joy, and our paths through flowers.

                                        THOMAS HARDY

*When you are really raging at the blows that seem, undeservedly, to have
been dealt out to you by God, by fate, or almost by a throw of the dice,
then the powerful Book of Job may be in line with your feelings. Job, in
chapter after chapter, rails against God for unmerited suffering. This
passage, from the* Good News Bible, *shows Job's totally negative feelings
most vividly. English translations of the Book of Job vary more than those
of almost any other book of the Bible, but the* Good News Bible *may
seem especially lucid to those who are asking, in anguish, 'Why, oh why?'
When you come to the magnificence of chapter 38, however, you might
want to read the majestic words of the* Authorised Version. *God never
once tells Job that he sent the sufferings to try or test him. He waits until
almost the end of the book, and then launches out into a thundering
statement of his unlimited power, might and majesty.*

            We are all born weak and helpless
            All lead the same short, troubled
                life.
            We grow and wither as quickly as
                flowers;
                we disappear like shadows.
            Will you even look at me, God
                or put me on trial and judge me?

Nothing clean can ever come
from anything as unclean as man.
The length of his life is decided
beforehand –
the number of months he will live.
You have settled it, and it can't be
changed.
Look away from him and leave him
alone;
let him enjoy his hard life – if he can.

There is hope for a tree that has been
cut down;
it can come back to life and sprout.
Even though its roots grow old,
and its stump dies in the ground,
with water it will sprout like a young
plant.
But a man dies, and that is the end
of him;
he dies, and where is he then?

Like rivers that stop running,
and lakes that go dry,
people die, never to rise.
They will never wake up while the sky
endures;
they will never stir from their sleep.

I wish you would hide me in the world
of the dead;
let me be hidden until your anger is
over,
and then set a time to remember me.
If a man dies, can he come back to
life?
But I will wait for better times,
wait till this time of trouble is ended.
Then you will call, and I will answer,
and you will be pleased with me, your
creature.

> Then you will watch every step I take,
> but you will not keep track of my
> sins.
> You will forgive them and put them
> away;
> you will wipe out all the wrongs I
> have done.
>
> There comes a time when mountains
> fall
> and solid cliffs are moved away.
> Water will wear down rocks,
> and heavy rain will wash away the
> soil;
> so you destroy man's hope for life.
> You overpower a man and send him
> away for ever;
> his face is twisted in death.
> His sons win honour, but he never
> knows it,
> nor is he told when they are disgraced.
> He feels only the pain of his own body
> and the grief of his own mind.

GOOD NEWS BIBLE; JOB 14:1–22

You might like to look at the short chapter on Job in Harold Kushner's memorable book 'When Bad Things Happen to Good People', which is especially addressed to those who are suffering or bereaved. This passage gives part of Rabbi Kushner's assessment of the meaning of the Book of Job.

In a way, it was comforting to believe in an all-wise, all-powerful God who guaranteed fair treatment and happy endings, who reassured us that everything happened for a reason, even as life was easier for us when we could believe that our parents were wise enough to know what to do and strong enough to make everything turn out right. But it was comforting the way the religion of Job's friends was comforting: it worked only as long as we did not take the problems of innocent victims seriously. When we have met Job, when we have *been* Job, we cannot believe in that sort of God any longer without giving up our own right to feel angry, to feel that we have been treated badly by life.

From that perspective, there ought to be a sense of relief in coming to the conclusion that God is not doing this to us. If God is a God of justice and not of power, then He can still be on our side when bad things happen to us. He can know that we are good and honest people who deserve better. Our misfortunes are none of His doing, and so we can turn to Him for help. Our question will not be Job's question 'God, why are You doing this to me?' but rather 'God, see what is happening to me. Can You help me?' We will turn to God, not to be judged or forgiven, not to be rewarded or punished, but to be strengthened and comforted.

If we have grown up, as Job and his friends did, believing in an all-wise, all-powerful, all-knowing God, it will be hard for us, as it was hard for them, to change our way of thinking about Him (as it was hard for us, when we were children, to realize that our parents were not all-powerful, that a broken toy had to be thrown out because they *could not* fix it, not because they did not want to). But if we can bring ourselves to acknowledge that there are some things God does not control, many good things become possible.

We will be able to turn to God for things He can do to help us, instead of holding on to unrealistic expectations of Him which will never come about. The Bible, after all, repeatedly speaks of God as the special protector of the poor, the widow, and the orphan, without raising the question of how it happened that they became poor, widowed, or orphaned in the first place.

We can maintain our own self-respect and sense of goodness without having to feel that God has judged us and condemned us. We can be angry at what has happened to us, without feeling that we are angry at God. More than that, we can recognize our anger at life's unfairness, our instinctive compassion at seeing people suffer, as coming from God who teaches us to be angry at injustice and to feel compassion for the afflicted. Instead of feeling that we are opposed to God, we can feel that our indignation is God's anger at unfairness working through us, that when we cry out, we are still on God's side, and He is still on ours.

HAROLD KUSHNER

Whatever the circumstances, we need somehow to find a meaning in the life and the death of a lost person. Some find it in the idea of a pattern that is not – or not yet – visible to us. The following verses, sometimes entitled 'The Weaver', are cherished by many bereaved people.

Man's life is laid in the loom of Time
To a pattern he does not see,
While the Weaver works and the shuttles fly
Till the doom of eternity.

Some shuttles are filled with silver thread,
And some with threads of gold;
While often but the darker hue
Is all that they may hold.

But the Weaver watches with skilful eye
Each shuttle fly to and fro,
And sees the pattern so deftly wrought
As the loom works slow and sure.

God surely planned that pattern,
Each thread – the dark and the fair –
Was chosen by His master skill
And placed in the web with care.

He only knows the beauty
And guides the shuttles which hold
The threads so unattractive
As well as the threads of gold.

Not till the loom is silent,
And the shuttles cease to fly
Shall God unroll the pattern
And explain the reason why.

The dark threads are as needful
In the Weaver's skilful hand
As the threads of gold and silver
In the pattern that He has planned.

                                    AUTHOR UNKNOWN

*Where the death was untimely or an accident, it is often especially hard
to discern some meaning in it. In a notable passage from 'When Bad
Things Happen to Good People', Rabbi Kushner suggests that some
of us may not want to go on trying, but should perhaps take a different
course:*

Let me suggest that the bad things that happen to us in our lives
do not have a meaning when they happen to us. They do not
happen for any good reason which would cause us to accept them

willingly. But we can give them a meaning. We can redeem these tragedies from senselessness by imposing meaning on them. The question we should be asking is not, 'Why did this happen to me? What did I do to deserve this?' That is really an unanswerable, pointless question. A better question would be, 'Now that this has happened to me, what am I going to do about it?' . . .

We . . . need to get over the questions that focus on the past and on the pain – 'why did this happen to me?' – and ask instead the question which opens doors to the future: 'Now that this has happened, what shall I do about it?' . . .

The facts of life and death are neutral. We, by our responses, give suffering either a positive or a negative meaning. Illness, accidents, human tragedies kill people. But they do not necessarily kill life or faith. If the death and suffering of someone we love makes us bitter, jealous, against all religion, and incapable of happiness, *we* turn the person who died into one of the 'devil's martyrs'. If suffering and death in someone close to us brings us to explore the limits of our capacity for strength and love and cheerfulness, if it leads us to discover sources of consolation we never knew before, then *we* make the person into a witness for the affirmation of life rather than its rejection.

This means . . . that there is one thing we can still do for those we loved and lost. We could not keep them alive. Perhaps we could not even significantly lessen their pain. But the one crucial thing we can do for them after their death is to let them be witnesses for God and for life, rather than, by our despair and loss of faith, making them 'the devil's martyrs'. The dead depend on us for their redemption and their immortality.

HAROLD KUSHNER

Dreams, and daytime visions of seeing a person, can be especially vivid in bereavement and are, of course, cruelly poignant when they bring back for a short period of bliss the person who is lost. Later on, the power of a dream can also reveal that some sharp emotional pain is still there, at a time when you think you have recovered.

Dreams in bereavement seem to have a psychological purpose. While much of the grief work in early bereavement is a kind of searching, the dream can be a temporary, mitigating finding. Quite quickly one realizes that it is only an illusion, and so one is back to pining and searching again. The intensity of this process will diminish eventually and will no

*longer trouble you much; but it will take a long time, and progress may
be erratic.*

This comes from Helen Waddell's 'Medieval Latin Lyrics'. *It is a
translation of a poem by Petronius Arbiter.*

> Dreams, dreams that mock us with their flitting shadows,
> They come not from the temples of the gods,
> They send them not, the powers of the air.
> Each man makes his own dreams. The body lies
> Quiet in sleep, what time the mind set free
> Follows in darkness what is sought by day.
> He who makes kingdoms quake for fear and sends
> Unhappy cities ruining in fire,
> Sees hurtling blows and broken fighting ranks
> And death of kings and sodden battle fields.
> The lawyer sees the judge, the crowded court,
> The miser hides his coin, digs buried treasure,
> The hunter shakes the forests with his hounds,
> The sailor rescues from the sea his ship,
> Or drowning, clings to it. Mistress to lover
> Writes a love-letter: the adulteress
> Yields in her sleep, and in his sleep the hound
> Is hot upon the traces of the hare.
> The wounds of the unhappy in the night
> Do but prolong their pain.

HELEN WADDELL

*Here is another of Arthur Waley's atmospheric translations from the
Chinese.*

> At night I dreamt I was back in Ch'ang-an;
> I saw again the faces of old friends.
> And in my dreams, under an April sky,
> They led me by the hand to wander in the spring
>   winds.
> Together we came to the village of Peace and
>   Quiet;
> We stopped our horses at the gate of Yuan Chen.
> Yuan Chen was sitting all alone;
> When he saw me coming, a smile came to his
>   face.

He pointed back at the flowers in the western
  court;
Then opened wine in the northern summer-
  house.
He seemed to be saying that neither of us had
  changed;
He seemed to be regretting that joy will not stay;
That our souls had met only for a little while,
To part again with hardly time for greeting.
I woke up and thought him still at my side;
I put out my hand; there was nothing there at all.

ARTHUR WALEY

*All bereaved people face the problem of revisiting places that hold very
special memories from the past. Do you avoid the place for a long time,
or for ever, for fear of the searing separation pain it might bring on? Or
do you hope to exorcize the fear and, indeed, possibly feel renewed
closeness by going there quickly?*

*Thomas Hardy, in his seventies, is here writing about his first wife.
How vividly he expresses the totally special quality of the place for two
people, its ordinariness for anyone else.*

At Castle Boterel

As I drive to the junction of lane and highway,
  And the drizzle bedrenches the waggonette,
I look behind at the fading byway,
  And see on its slope, now glistening wet,
    Distinctly yet

Myself and a girlish form benighted
  In dry March weather. We climb the road
Beside a chaise. We had just alighted
  To ease the sturdy pony's load
    When he sighed and slowed.

What we did as we climbed, and what we talked of
  Matters not much, nor to what it led, –
Something that life will not be balked of
  Without rude reason till hope is dead,
    and feeling fled.

It filled but a minute. But was there ever
   A time of such quality, since or before,
In that hill's story? To one mind never,
   Though it has been climbed, foot-swift, foot-sore,
      By thousands more.

Primaeval rocks form the road's steep border,
   And much have they faced there, first and last,
Of the transitory in Earth's long order;
   But what they record in colour and cast
      Is – that we two passed.

And to me, though Time's unflinching rigour,
   In mindless rote, has ruled from sight
The substance now, one phantom figure
   Remains on the slope, as when that night
      Saw us alight.

I look and see it there, shrinking, shrinking,
   I look back at it amid the rain
For the very last time; for my sand is sinking,
   And I shall traverse old love's domain
      Never again.

                                        THOMAS HARDY

In April

      I am come to the threshold of a spring
      Where there will be nothing
      To stand between me and the smite
      Of the martin's scooping flight,
      Between me and the halloo
      Of the first cuckoo.
      'As you hear the first cuckoo,
      So you will be all summer through.'
      This year I shall hear it naked and alone;
      And lengthening days and strengthening sun will
         show
      Me my solitary shadow
      My cypressed shadow – but no;

My Love, I was not alone: in my mind I was
   talking with you
When I heard the first cuckoo,
And gentle as thistledown his call was blown.

SYLVIA TOWNSEND WARNER

*In Daphne du Maurier's 'The Rebecca Notebook', which describes the
making of that ever-popular novel, there are also some other autobiograph-
ical essays, including a telling one on her reactions to widowhood.*

The old adage, Time heals all wounds, is only true if there is no
suppuration within. To be bitter, to lament unceasingly, 'Why did
this have to happen to him?' makes the wound fester; the mind,
renewing the stab, causes the wound to bleed afresh. It is hard,
very hard, not to be bitter in the early days, not to blame doctors,
hospitals, drugs, that failed to cure. Harder still for the woman
whose husband died not by illness but by accident, who was cut
short in full vigour, in the prime of life, killed perhaps in a car
crash returning home from work. The first instinct is to seek
revenge upon the occupants of the other car, themselves unhurt,
whose selfish excess of speed caused the disaster. Yet this is no
answer to grief. All anger, all reproach, turns inwards upon itself.
The infection spreads, pervading the mind and body.

I would say to those who mourn – and I can only speak from
my own experience – look upon each day that comes as a challenge,
as a test of courage. The pain will come in waves, some days
worse than others, for no apparent reason. Accept the pain. Do
not suppress it. Never attempt to hide grief from yourself. Little
by little, just as the deaf, the blind, the handicapped develop with
time an extra sense to balance disability, so the bereaved, the
widowed, will find new strength, new vision, born of the very
pain and loneliness which seem, at first, impossible to master. I
address myself more especially to the middle-aged who, like
myself, look back to over thirty years or more of married life and
find it hardest to adapt. The young must, of their very nature,
heal sooner than ourselves.

DAPHNE DU MAURIER

Lost in Despair

Lately I have been letting my life
Fall into pieces about me.
All the old familiar ways have become meaningless.
I have been lost in despair's dark depths.
I have been lost in a forest of ills,
Wandering alone and calling for help,
I have looked to death as an escape
From the intolerable agony within.
Now it is time for me to turn from death
And chart another path.
Girding myself with courage and with hope,
I must find new tasks
And make a new beginning from an old and finished ending.

MARJORIE PIZER

Overwhelmed

When I feel overwhelmed by destruction,
Let me go down to the sea.
Let me sit by the immeasurable ocean
And watch the surf
Beating in and running out all day and all night.
Let me sit by the sea
And have the bitter sea winds
Slap my cheeks with their cold, damp hands
Until I am sensible again.
Let me look at the sky at night
And let the stars tell me
Of limitless horizons and unknown universes
Until I am grown calm and strong once more.

MARJORIE PIZER

3

The death of infants, children and young people

She asked life of thee, and thou gavest her a long life, even for ever and ever.

ON A MEMORIAL IN GREWELTHORPE VILLAGE CHURCH, YORKSHIRE, TO A GIRL WHO DIED AGED SEVENTEEN

As befits this most searing area, there are sharp contrasts of approach in the prose extracts and poems: between a relentless despair and a quiet and, perhaps, even joyful hope; between the most painful sense of emptiness and waste and a strong feeling of purpose in that short life, with or without a firm belief in immortality.

So there is much pain in this chapter, and some consolation and even joy. The pain may be especially sharp when the extract mirrors your own experience. You may want to skip the bits that hurt too much; but they might read rather differently in a few months' time.

From **Men's Search for Meaning**

We cannot judge a biography by its length, by the number of pages in it; we must judge by the richness of the contents . . . Sometimes the 'unfinisheds' are among the most beautiful symphonies.

VICTOR FRANKL

For a Child Born Dead

What ceremony can we fit
You into now? If you had come
Out of a warm and noisy room
To this, there'd be an opposite
For us to know you by. We could
Imagine you in lively mood

And then look at the other side,
The mood drawn out of you, the breath
Defeated by the power of death.
But we have never seen you stride
Ambitiously the world we know.
You could not come and yet you go.

But there is nothing now to mar
Your clear refusal of our world.
Not in our memories can we mould
You or distort your character.
Then all our consolation is
That grief can be as pure as this.

ELIZABETH JENNINGS

*Harriet Sarnott Schiff wrote a book about her own experiences called
'The Bereaved Parent'. The extract below is one of the most positive
in the book, but many other passages may provide insight and support.*

You probably never thought you could live through your child's
funeral. What could have been more dreadful? But you did.

Certainly surviving all the grief you felt seemed impossible.
Those days and nights of crying, exhaustion, and pain were almost
beyond endurance. You were certain, at times, you would never
get past that time in your life. But you did.

There were times you felt great guilt because somehow you had
not filled the role of 'parent' as society interprets the role. You
were unable to save your child and keep it alive. As that cold,
clammy feeling would come over you and your back would prickle
thinking about what you could have done differently, you were
sunk into such a pit of grieving that you never dreamed it would
be possible to go on. But you did.

Often, you were beset with anger and a feeling of powerlessness
because events that should have been in your control simply were

not. You did not think you could overcome these feelings – especially the hopelessness that accompanied them. But you can.

Just when you needed your mate most, you would find he or she could help you least. You expected comfort from someone incapable of comforting. You argued. Sometimes you even hated. You never thought you would rise from the bottom of the well of sorrow. But you can.

You thought never again could you take an interest in the world and retain friendships and attend weddings and happy occasions for other people's children. You were certain you could never live through the trauma. But you will.

There was no doubt in your mind that you never again could enjoy yourself. Never want to travel. Never give parties – or attend them. Never have fun. You would only be sorrowful and certainly you would never laugh. Above all, not laugh. But you will.

And most of all, you were sure it would be impossible for you to function as a whole human being not buffeted by the waves of sorrow that swept over you in the early days of your tragedy. But you will.

You will do all that and you will do more.

HARRIET SARNOTT SCHIFF

Death of a Son
(who died in a mental hospital, aged one)

Something has ceased to come along with me.
Something like a person: something very like one.
And there was no nobility in it
Or anything like that.

Something was there like a one year
Old house, dumb as stone. While the near buildings
Sang like birds and laughed
Understanding the pact

They were to have with silence. But he
Neither sang nor laughed. He did not bless silence
Like bread, with words.
He did not forsake silence.

But rather, like a house in mourning
Kept the eye turned in to watch the silence while
The other houses like birds
Sang around him.

And the breathing silence neither
Moved nor was still.

I have seen stones: I have seen brick
But this house was made up of neither bricks nor stone
But a house of flesh and blood
With flesh of stone

And bricks for blood. A house
Of stones and blood in breathing silence with the other
Birds singing crazy on its chimneys.
But this was silence,

This was something else, this was
Hearing and speaking though he was a house drawn
Into silence, this was
Something religious in his silence,

Something shining in his quiet,
This was different, this was altogether something else:
Though he never spoke, this
Was something to do with death.

And then slowly the eye stopped looking
Inward. The silence rose and became still.
The look turned to the outer place and stopped,
With the birds still shrilling around him.
And as if he could speak

He turned over on his side with his one year
Red as a wound
He turned over as if he could be sorry for this
And out of his eyes two great tears rolled, like stones,
and he died.

JON SILKIN

Prayer for the Little Daughter between Death and Burial

Now you are standing face to face with the clear light
believe in it
Now you have gone back into where air comes from
hold fast to it
Now you have climbed to the top of the topless tower
and there are no stairs down
and the only way is flight past the edge of the world
do not remember us

Like the new moon in the sky of the shortest day
you came to us
as the candles burnt with a steady light behind misty windows
you whispered to us
as the singers moved behind doors of un-attainable rooms
you burst in on us
Lady of the shortest day, silent upon the threshold
carrying green branches

Lady of the crown of light going into clear light
be safe on your journey
Bright lady of the dark day, who pushed back the darkness
say nothing to us
as we plod through the frozen field
going from somewhere to somewhere
do not speak to us
as we stand at the centre of the frozen lake
and trees of cloud stand over us
forget us

When we come to you we shall find you
who have seen Persephone
you whom our mothers called Lady of the city
will welcome us with tapers, and believe in us
When small harsh birds bubble and pump in our nude trees
and water will rush and gush through the slippery street
and two skies will look at each other
one of air and one below
of water
you will rest with us, and of us:

Lady of the shortest day
watch over our daughter
whom we commit to the grass

DIANA SCOTT

The loss of a child

. . . the deceased has removed into a better country, and bounded away to a happier inheritance; . . . thou hast not lost thy son, but bestowed him henceforward in an inviolable spot. Say not then, I pray thee, I am no longer called 'father', for why art thou no longer called so, when thy son abideth? For surely thou didst not part with thy child, nor lose thy son? Rather thou hast gotten him, and hast him in greater safety. Wherefore, no longer shalt thou be called 'father' here only, but also in heaven; so that thou hast not lost the title 'father', but hast gained it in a nobler sense; for henceforth thou shalt be called father not of a mortal child, but of an immortal . . . For think not, because he is not present, that therefore he is lost; for had he been absent in a foreign land, the title of thy relationship had not gone from thee with his body.

ST JOHN CHRYSOSTOM

Some of the most stark, most unrelenting thoughts are here in these extracts from a poem by James Russell Lowell. They may be too hard for the moment.

> Yes, faith is a goodly anchor;
> When skies are sweet as a psalm,
> At the bows it lolls so stalwart,
> In its bluff, broad-shouldered calm . . .
>
> But, after the shipwreck, tell me
> What help in its iron thews,
> Still true to the broken hawser,
> Deep down among sea-weed and ooze?
>
> In the breaking gulfs of sorrow,
> When the helpless feet stretch out
> And find in the deeps of darkness
> No footing so solid as doubt,

Then better one spar of Memory
One broken plank of the Past,
That our human heart may cling to,
Though hopeless of shore at last! . . .

Immortal? I feel it and know it,
Who doubts it of such as she?
But that is the pang's very secret, –
Immortal away from me.

There's a narrow ridge in the graveyard
Would scarce stay a child in his race,
But to me and my thought it is wider
Than the star-sown vague of Space.

Your logic, my friend, is perfect,
Your moral most drearily true;
But, since the earth clashed on her coffin,
I keep hearing that, and not you.

Console if you will, I can bear it;
'Tis a well-meant alms of breath;
But not all the preaching since Adam
Has made Death other than Death.

It is pagan; but wait till you feel it, –
That jar of our earth, that dull shock
When the ploughshare of deeper passion
Tears down to our primitive rock.

Communion in spirit! Forgive me,
But I, who am earthly and weak,
Would give all my incomes from dreamland
For a touch of her hand on my cheek . . .

JAMES RUSSELL LOWELL

Letter sent to Alix and George Reindorp

It was with great sorrow that I heard today of the death of your child. The religion of Christ was always sincere and clear-sighted. He refused to obscure the fact that tragedy was tragedy; and wept at the grave of Lazarus. It must therefore be in the circumference of His love that we recognize our torn hearts when we part with a child who has held all that was best in us in fee.

The fact that He could weep over the death of a loved one when He knew that in so short a time He was going to supply the answer which made hope the sequel to every tragedy, even the tragedy of sin, surely shows that here in time and space, grief and hope can come to us side by side.

Thus I pray it may be with you and your wife.

It has been given to me to see our progress to God as a road divided in the middle by a low wall, which we call death. Whatever our age or stage of development, or relationship with other human beings, there is no real change involved in crossing the low wall. We simply continue in a parallel course with those who loved us in our development and relationship. I do not believe that God has altered one whit your responsibility or service for your child.

I do believe that she will grow side by side with you, in spirit, as she would have done on earth; and that your prayer and love will serve her development as they would have done on earth. There is nothing static about the other life.

The difficulty is that our spiritual sight is so little developed compared with our earthly sight. We cannot watch the development and growth as we could on earth. Yet much can be done by faith, by the realization that what we hope is true, and that we can train our minds and imaginations to think in terms of truths, even if they are pictured in earthly forms. The companionship which was given you, you still have. The growth to which you look forward will still be yours to watch over and care for.

You will be much in my prayers at this time. What I have written I know to be true and I pray that you may be enabled to live in that truth and to find the answer to your tragedy.

Sarah, aged seven

In the days shortly before her death, she would lie curled up in a chair, half-dozing, half-watching us as we lived out our lives around her. Smiling, she would say; 'I'm so happy, I feel I've got arms tight round me.' Her death was the most exciting moment of my life. Deep in the almost overwhelming pain and grief of her going I was still conscious of a great joy and triumph; joy that she had not been destroyed by her suffering, that she was still confident and reassured; joy that we were able to hand her back into and on to the greatest Love of all; joy that this was not really the end. I felt a very real sense of a new birth – more painful but as exciting as her first one seven years earlier. There was an inexplicable but unshakable knowledge that all was indeed well.

JANE DAVIES

Lament for Glen
(Killed in a motor-bike accident, aged nineteen)

> The splendid youth is dead and is no more,
> And who shall comfort those who are left?
> Who shall comfort the mother who has lost her son?
> Who shall comfort the sisters who have lost a brother?
> Who shall comfort the friends who have lost a friend?
> And who shall comfort the father?
> There is no comfort for those who are grieving
> For faith is not enough
> To assuage the tearing wound of sudden death.
> O let me not drown in the flood of grief
> For all young men who died before their time
> And for this one so newly dead.
> O let me catch the raft of life again
> And not be swept away
> Into the darkest depths of grief and loss.

MARJORIE PIZER

How does the familiar quotation below find its way into this chapter? At first glance it seems inextricably linked with the war dead and the cere-monies of Remembrance Day. But I am told by one of the staff at Great Ormond Street Children's Hospital that many of the families who lose a child find these lines completely relevant to their situation, and most comforting.

We Will Remember Them

> They shall grow not old, as we that are left grow old:
> Age shall not weary them, nor the years condemn.
> At the going down of the sun and in the morning
> We will remember them.

LAURENCE BINYON

*Christopher Leach's book 'Letter to a Younger Son' is really a diary
of the weeks and months after his elder boy Jonathan died; but it is
addressed to his other son, Martin. Some readers may find parts of it
extremely raw and stark, perhaps especially where it reflects their own
experience, but it remains one of the most thoughtful and beautifully
written books by a parent whose child has died.*

Death is built into us. The last fail-safe. It is inherent in our birth;
and it is the border to our lives. There may be a time in the
future when death itself will die: when for every failing organ, a
replacement is speedily grafted into the system. But there is something repugnant in the concept of an unnaturally extended life. A
man needs to die as well as to live. He needs to re-enter the flow;
or to know Heaven or Hell; or to go into oblivion: what you will.
I do not believe life is a preparation for death: that old grey
teaching. Life is a preparation for the fullest enjoyment of the next
minute; but to be aware of death is to appreciate the never-to-
come-again worth of that minute, free of the dark.

That is one of the lessons of Jonathan's death, or of any other
death, man, lover, cat, hare, or rose.

Even if his death was fortuitous, what arises from it is not. In
other words, we construct from our disasters the means of dealing
with that disaster. And, thus armoured, move on.

I believe that Jonathan – *as Jonathan my son* – now exists nowhere
but in my own mind. I could be quite wrong: but that is what my
reason tells me – and I have not the faith to believe otherwise.
Others tell me to leave reason aside: that the spiritual life is
comprehended by other factors, never by the intellect. But I love
reason; and the idea of my personality, or any other, continuing
for eternity, appears impossible; and limiting: I want to try other
universes, other forms. If I close my eyes I can see Jonathan. He
will never age. A child will accompany my last minute, as he now
accompanies my every breath. All who live with the memory of
a dead loved one feel a measure of guilt. Not enough was said;
not enough was done. It is a natural, human emotion: born of a
certainty that that face, that body, will never be seen again – as
that body, that loved face. . . .

I have not accepted his death. Is any death acceptable? That of
the pain-racked, perhaps; of those who have had enough; the
tortured who gladly seek that sweet oblivion. Though others tell
me he lives elsewhere, I believe he does not. Not as Jonathan: the
individual I helped to make. What has been given back (taken

back) is an essence of life which has no name, is no longer housed in anything I would recognize. The form has gone. I have to live the rest of my life in the knowledge that all I have is eleven years of memories; a few photographs (which I cannot look at, yet); and assorted drawings and writings which hint at what might have been; and are evidence of some delight and awareness at being human.

What is the worth?

The worth is an enlargement of myself. I am not speaking of the nobility of suffering. I have always had a horror of the self-inflicted wound – the pain pilgrims feel, going on their knees up a rough track, towards a clean, kissed shrine. I see no merit in sainthood; and the Stations of the Cross have no place in my world.

But an unexpected window has opened; and beyond it is a new landscape which, though still marked by withered trees and gaunt winter-struck gardens is, even as I watch, slowly losing some of its bruising chill; and, ironically, may in time be visited, for the sake of its own strange beauty, as often and as easily as that other country: its pulsing, colourful, summerful neighbour, the land of the living . . .

I had planned to finish this letter on the anniversary of Jonathan's death. I have in fact finished it three weeks earlier. Life, and growth, for humanity is never that well-rounded. Things are finished before their time; or in a time which runs on other rules than ours.

And so, Martin, I come to an end. You know a little more about me than when you began reading. Yet I am still hidden, even to myself: life is a shifting, tremulous thing, elusive as quicksilver. Part of me resides in you; another part is scattered with the ashes that was Jonathan's shell. Being human, I am still hurt. Being human, I am not reconciled; yet part of me soars.

If there is a light after the dark of death, by the glow of which I shall know and be known – fused to the lost part of me, all tragedies explained, all wounds healed (that old human longing for love's extension) – then I am content to wait and see.

But I live believing the opposite: that I have been granted a certain time to walk about this Earth, and to take a look at its marvels and its follies – and perhaps contribute to both – and what I do *matters*: if only because I can do no other – being set going, my heart ticking, my blood running. And then a transformation, the nature of which I do not know, but trust, since all humanity has gone before, and will go: borne upon an air I have loved, circling my home, the Earth, and moving on . . .

But I am in no hurry: I have things to do. Death can wait a while.

Or not wait.

CHRISTOPHER LEACH

4

Prayers from many sources

Give them rest with the devout and the just, in the place of the pasture of rest and of refreshment, of waters in the paradise of delight, whence grief and pain and sighing have fled away.

FROM AN EARLY CHRISTIAN PRAYER

This book, and especially this chapter, tries to respect the fact that bereaved people come from every religious tradition: many are tentative in their beliefs, many are agnostic, and some are atheists. Like the Quakers, I would not want to foist Christian comfort on to those who are unreceptive to it either temporarily or entirely. All the prayers printed here, however, do encompass concepts which, potentially, apply to very many human beings suffering the emptiness and travail of bereavement.

I hope that all will find some help here, partly because so many of us have an intuitive sense of immanence of some kind, and partly because, in Cardinal Hume's strong words, people are 'hungry for the truth about their own lives and the meaning of them'.

For some, the prayers here can be truly said and truly prayed – raised in the mind and heart to God, holding up to him the person who has died, and our own sorrow and desolation.

However they are used, it is hoped that these prayers will help bring inner peace.

An African's Prayer

I have no other helper than you, no other father, I pray
  to you.
Only you can help me. My present misery is too great.
Despair grips me, and I am at my wit's end.
O Lord, Creator, Ruler of the World, Father,
I thank you that you have brought me through.

How strong the pain was – but you were stronger.
How deep the fall was – but you were even deeper.
How dark the night was – but you were the noonday
   sun in it.
You are our father, our mother, our brother, and our friend.

Prayer after a crushing bereavement

To me who am left to mourn his departure, grant that I may not
sorrow as one without hope for my beloved who sleeps in Thee;
but that, always remembering his courage, and the love that united
us on earth, I may begin again with new courage to serve Thee
more fervently who art the only source of true love and true
fortitude; that, when I have passed a few more days in this valley
of tears and in this shadow of death, supported by Thy rod and
staff, I may see him again, face to face, in those pastures and
amongst those waters of comfort where, I trust, he already walks
with Thee. Oh Shepherd of the Sheep, have pity upon this
darkened soul of mine!

R. H. BENSON

Prayer of St Francis de Sales

Do not look forward to what might happen tomorrow; the same
everlasting Father who cares for you today, will take care of you
tomorrow and every day. Either He will shield you from suffering
or He will give you unfailing strength to bear it. Be at peace, then,
and put aside all anxious thoughts and imaginings.

*Bede Jarrett (1881–1934) was an English Dominican preacher, historian
and essayist. This prayer, found by him, is becoming increasingly well
known. Joyce Grenfell very much appreciated the phrase 'death is only
an horizon' and mentioned it several times in letters to friends.*

We seem to give them back to thee, O God, who gavest them to
us. Yet as thou didst not lose them in giving, so we do not lose
them by their return. Not as the world giveth, givest thou, O
lover of souls. What thou givest, thou takest not away, for what
is thine is ours also if we are thine. And life is eternal and love is

immortal, and death is only an horizon, and an horizon is nothing save the limit of our sight. Lift us up, strong Son of God, that we may see further; cleanse our eyes that we may see more clearly; draw us closer to thyself that we may know ourselves to be nearer to our loved ones who are with thee. And while thou dost prepare a place for us, prepare us also for that happy place, that where thou art we may be also for evermore. Amen.

ANONYMOUS

A Prayer

Clother of the lily, Feeder of the sparrow,
　　Father of the fatherless, dear Lord,
Tho' Thou set me as a mark against Thine arrow,
　　As a prey unto Thy sword,
As a plough'd-up field beneath Thy harrow,
　　As a captive in Thy cord,
Let that cord be love; and some day make my narrow
　　Hallow'd bed according to Thy Word. Amen.

CHRISTINA ROSSETTI

★　★　★

Keep me in thy love
As thou wouldest that all should be kept
　　in mine.
May everything in this my being
Be directed to thy glory
And may I never despair.
For I am under thy hand,
And in thee is all power and goodness.

DAG HAMMARSKJÖLD

★　★　★

He said not: thou shalt not be tempested, thou shalt not be travailed, thou shalt not be afflicted; but he said: thou shalt not be overcome.

MOTHER JULIAN OF NORWICH

Seventeenth-century prayer

We beseech thee, Lord,
Remember all for good:
Have pity upon all, O sovereign Lord . . .
　　Nourish our infants,
　　Lead forward our youth,
　　Sustain our aged,

Comfort the faint-hearted,
　　Gather together the dispersed,
　　Restore the wanderers,
　　Set free the troubled with unclean spirits,
Travel with the travellers,
　　Stand forth for the widow and widower,
　　Shield the orphan,
　　Rescue the captive and heal the sick.

Remember, O God, all who need thy great compassion,
And upon all pour out thy rich pity.

For thou, Lord, art the succour of the succourless,
　　The hope of the hopeless,
　　The Saviour of the tempest-tossed,
　　The harbour of the voyager,
The physician of the sick.

For thou knowest every man and his petition,
Every house and its need,
Being the God of all spirits and of all flesh.

                                        LANCELOT ANDREWES

                    ★　★　★

God, omit not this man from Thy covenant,
And the many evils which he in the body committed,
That he cannot this night enumerate.
　　The many evils that he in the body committed,
　　That he cannot this night enumerate.

Be this soul on Thine own arm, O Christ,
Thou King of the City of Heaven,
And since Thine it was, O Christ, to buy the soul,
At the time of the balancing of the beam,
At the time of the bringing in the judgement,
Be it now on Thine own right hand,
　　Oh! on Thine own right hand.

And be the holy Michael, king of angels,
Coming to meet the soul,
And leading it home
To the heaven of the Son of God
  The holy Michael, high king of angels,
  Coming to meet the soul,
  And leading it home
  To the heaven of the Son of God.

AN ANCIENT GAELIC PRAYER

I Weep in Love

I am glad, Lord, for I wept today.
And I hid my tears inside my handkerchief.
Still my eyes were burning, and my head got hot;
My heart was beating fast and I felt weak,
Solemn thoughts rose up from my mind,
And a note of thankfulness played its melody in my being.
Why? I do not know.
I know that drops of tears which I hid in my kerchief,
Have been a stepping stone for me to thee,
Lord, I cry, make me weep,
And give me tears to flow;
Thy loving touch transforms my grief
Into joy, and peace, and I weep in love –
I am glad, Lord, for I wept today.

MEDITATION BY AN INDIAN CHRISTIAN

★ ★ ★

Eternal and most glorious God, suffer me not so to undervalue
myself as to give away my soul, Thy soul, Thy dear and precious
soul, for nothing. All the world is nothing, if the soul must be
given for it. Preserve therefore my soul, O Lord, because it belongs
to Thee. Preserve also my body because it belongs to my soul.
Thou alone dost steer my boat through all its voyage, but hast a
more special care of it, when it comes to a narrow current, or to
a dangerous fall of waters. Thou hast a care of the preservation of
my body in all the ways of my life. Enlarge Thy Providence
towards me so far that no illness or agony may shake and benumb

the soul. Do Thou so make my bed in all my sickness that, being used to Thy hand, I may be content with any bed of Thy making. Amen.

JOHN DONNE (adapted)

★   ★   ★

'Almighty Father, Thy love is like a great sea that girdles the earth. Out of the deep we come to float a while upon its surface. We cannot sound its depth nor tell its greatness, only we know it never faileth. The winds that blow over us are the breathing of Thy Spirit; the sun that lights and warms us is Thy truth. Now Thou dost suffer us to sail calm seas; now Thou dost buffet us with storms of trouble; on the crest of waves of sorrow Thou dost raise us, but it is Thy love that bears us up; in the trough of desolation Thou dost sink us that we may see nought but Thy love on every side. And when we pass into the deep again the waters of Thy love encompass and enfold us. The foolish call them the waters of misery and death; those who have heard the whisper of Thy spirit know them for the boundless ocean of eternal life and love.

ANONYMOUS

From Gitanjali

When the heart is hard and parched up, come upon me with a shower of mercy.

When grace is lost from life, come with a burst of song.

When tumultuous work raises its din on all sides shutting me out from beyond, come to me, my Lord of silence, with thy peace and rest.

When my beggarly heart sits crouched, shut up in a corner, break upon the door, my king, and come with the ceremony of a king.

When desire blinds the mind with delusion and dust, O thou holy One, thou wakeful, come with thy light and thy thunder.

RABINDRANATH TAGORE

King Charles I copied out this prayer by Sir Philip Sidney for his own use.

O All-seeing Light and eternal Life of all things, to whom nothing is either so great that it may resist, or so small that it is contemned; look upon my misery with Thine eye of mercy, and let Thine infinite power vouchsafe to limit out some proportion of deliverance unto me, as to Thee shall seem most convenient. Let not injury, O Lord, triumph over me, and let my faults by Thy hand be corrected, and make not mine enemy the minister of Thy justice. But yet, O Lord, if, in Thy wisdom; this be the aptest chastisement for my inexcusable folly; if this low bondage be fittest for my over-high desires; and the pride of my not enough humble heart be thus to be broken, O Lord, I yield unto Thy will, and joyfully embrace what sorrow thou wilt have me suffer. Only this let me crave of Thee . . . that Thou wilt suffer some beams of Thy majesty to shine into my mind, that it may still depend confidently on Thee. Let calamity be the exercise, but not the overthrow of my virtue: let their power prevail, but prevail not to destruction . . . But, O Lord, let never their wickedness have such a hand, but that I may carry a pure mind in a pure body.

SIR PHILIP SIDNEY

★ ★ ★

O Lord, Jesus Christ, Who art as the Shadow of a Great Rock in a weary land, Who beholdest Thy weak creatures weary of labour, weary of pleasure, weary of hope deferred, weary of self; in Thine abundant compassion, and fellow-feeling with us, and unutterable tenderness, bring us, we pray Thee, unto Thy rest . . . Amen.

CHRISTINA ROSSETTI

The following lines are inscribed on a monument a few miles from Aviemore in Speyside, Scotland.

Let the Great Shepherd lead and by winding ways,
not without green pastures and still waters,
we shall climb insensibly and reach the tops
   of the everlasting hills,
where the winds are cool and the sight is glorious.

5

Is there life after death?

He that hath found some fledg'd bird's nest, may know
At first sight, if the bird be flown;
But what fair Well, or Grove he sings in now,
That is to him unknown.

HENRY VAUGHAN

Unless we are theologians, we do not often have the chance to use that dramatic word eschatology, *defined in the* 'Oxford Dictionary of the Christian Church' *as dealing with 'the final destiny both of the individual and of mankind in general'.*

If you studied, for ten years, the wealth of eschatological literature from every culture and every religion, you would still not come up with a selection that created a fair balance – a balance between inspired writing, passages that could become anchors for bereaved people, and writing that represented the most influential theological and philosophical ideas. In this selection the only criterion is that passages are known to have been helpful in bereavement, or we hope that they might be.

Some of the greatest writers on immortality are not represented here. Some beliefs are not represented at all, or only briefly. There is not a lot, for instance, about the idea of 'the sleep eternal, in an eternal night'. The bias is in favour of some sort of after-life, whether Christian, Hindu, secular or different again.

We crave for clues. There is great interest in reports of the experiences of people who have 'died' and been resuscitated (especially in Raymond Moody's 'Life after Life'*). The vast majority in the West who consider consciousness to be the product of the brain alone obviously cannot allow the possibility of its continuation after physical death. In the East it has always been different; and an excited minority in the West is seizing upon ideas about the after-life from ancient Oriental religions and philosophies. Some of these are startlingly in line with the latest theories in quantum-relativistic physics, and can be studied in Fritjof Capra's* 'The Tao of Physics'*.*

Some mainstream Christian thinkers, and the individualists, have recently been able to respond to and promote a grassroots upsurge in intuitive spirituality. George Orwell said in 1944 that belief in survival after death is 'enormously less widespread than it was'; but I believe this trend has been reversed since then.

And so this chapter carries many different concepts and images. I hope that all searching readers will find one or more poems or extracts which fit their outlook, and perhaps seem to be their heart on paper.

Towards the end of the chapter the extracts address themselves to the urgent problem of whether we shall see our loved ones again, in one way or another.

From **Gitanjali**

I have got my leave. Bid me farewell, my brothers!
I bow to you all and take my departure.
   Here I give back the keys of my door – and I give up
all claims to my house. I only ask for last kind words
from you.
   We were neighbours for long, but I received more
than I could give. Now the day has dawned and the
lamp that lit my dark corner is out. A summons has
come and I am ready for my journey.

RABINDRANATH TAGORE

The Funeral

People were following:
The family – some crying,
Some pretending to cry;
Friends – some grieving,
Some bored or chatting.

Leaving the cemetery, some of the family were sobbing: 'All is
finished.'

Others were sniffling: 'Come, come, my dear, courage, it's
   finished!'
Some friends murmured: 'Poor man, that's how we'll all finish.'
And others sighed in relief: 'Well, it's over.'

And I was thinking that everything was just beginning.

Yes, he had finished the last rehearsal, but the eternal show was
   just beginning.
The years of training were over, but the eternal work was about
   to commence.
He had just been born to life,
The real life,
Life that's going to last,
Life eternal.

As if there were dead people!
There are no dead people, Lord.
There are only the living, on earth and beyond.
Death is real, Lord,
But it's nothing but a moment,
A second, a step,
The step from provisional to permanent,
From temporal to eternal.
So in the death of the child the adolescent is born,
   from the caterpillar emerges the butterfly,
   from the grain the full-blown ear.

Death, grotesque character, bogey-man of little children, non-
   existent phantom,
I don't take you seriously,
But I am disgusted with you.
You terrify the world,
You frighten and deceive men,
And yet your only reason for existing is life, and you are not
   able to take from us those that we love.

But where are they, Lord, those that I have loved?
Are they in ecstasy, taken up with holy loving in harmony with
   the Trinity?

Are they tormented in the night, burning with desire to love
   with an infinite love?
Are they in despair, condemned to their own selves because they
   preferred themselves to others? Consumed with hate because
   they can no longer love?

Lord, my loved ones are near me.
I know that they live in the shadow.
My eyes can't see them because they have left for a moment their
   bodies as one leaves behind outmoded clothing.

Their souls, deprived of their disguise, no longer communicate
with me.

But in you, Lord, I hear them calling me.
I see them beckoning to me.
I hear them giving me advice.
For they are now more vividly present.
Before, our bodies touched but not our souls.
Now I meet them when I meet you.
I receive them when I receive you.
I love them when I love you.
O, my loved ones, eternally alive, who live in me,
Help me to learn thoroughly in this short life how to live
eternally.

Lord, I love you, and I want to love you more.
It's you who make love eternal, and I want to love eternally.

MICHEL QUOIST

From **The Apocrypha**

The souls of the righteous are in the hand of God, and there shall
no torment touch them.
In the sight of the unwise they seemed to die: and their departure
is taken for misery.
And their going from us to be utter destruction: but they are in
peace.
For though they be punished in the sight of men, yet is their
hope full of immortality.
And having been a little chastised, they shall be greatly rewarded:
for God proved them, and found them worthy for himself.

As gold in the furnace hath he tried them, and received them as
a burnt offering.
And in the time of their visitation they shall shine, and run to
and fro like sparks among the stubble.
They shall judge the nations, and have dominion over the people,
and their Lord shall reign for ever.
They that put their trust in him shall understand the truth: and
such as be faithful in love shall abide with him: for grace and
mercy is to his saints, and he hath care for his elect.

THE WISDOM OF SOLOMON 3:1

From **Bede's Ecclesiastical History**

I believe that the life of man as we know it upon earth can be compared with the rest of time, of which we know nothing, in the following way: when you are seated at table with your court and your officers in winter time, with your hall warmed by the central hearth, while outside the storms of rain or snow are raging everywhere, a sparrow may enter the building and swiftly fly through it; coming in by one door and soon leaving by another it does not feel the tempest while it is inside, but after a brief moment of peace it returns to the cold from which it came and is lost to your eyes. In the same way human life is a brief interlude: what came before and what follows is mystery. Therefore if this new teaching gives us some trustworthy clue, we should indeed become its disciples.

THE VENERABLE BEDE
(trans. Austin Whitaker)

Many bereaved people appreciate this poem, although its subject is 'A Nun takes the Veil'.

Heaven-Haven

> I have desired to go
>   Where springs not fail,
> To fields where flies no sharp and sided hail
>   And a few lilies blow.
>
> And I have asked to be
>   Where no storms come,
> Where the green swell is in the havens dumb,
>   And out of the swing of the sea.

GERARD MANLEY HOPKINS

This passage has been adapted into a prayer, but here is the original text from Donne's Sermons.

They shall awake as Jacob did, and say as Jacob said: Surely the Lord is in this place and this is no other but the house of God and the gate of heaven. And into that gate they shall enter and in that house they shall dwell, where there shall be no cloud nor sun, no darkness nor dazzling, but one equal light, no noise nor silence, but one equal music, no fears nor hopes, but one equal possession, no foes nor friends, but one equal communion and identity, no ends nor beginnings, but one equal eternity. Keep us O Lord so awake.

JOHN DONNE

Close, Mortal Eyes

> Close, mortal eyes: open, my eyes, in heaven
> On consolations that the poor devise,
> On the clay image and the candles seven
>   Close, mortal eyes.
>
> Open upon the plains of the merry land,
> Eternal eyes, on joy for ever whole:
> Return with tidings I shall understand,
>   Eyes of my soul.
>
> The soul has eyes: alas, she has no tongue,
> She has no word of all the mysteries,
> No syllable that may be said or sung.
>   Close, mortal eyes.

RUTH PITTER

What detailed speculations about an after-life do we have from Greek and Roman times, before Christianity impinged? Plato's view is well known and often quoted, but this passage of Cicero's, from his beautiful essay on old age, is perhaps less familiar.

I find this ripeness very welcome; in fact, as I approach death I seem to see the shore and believe I shall at last reach harbour after a long voyage . . . For as long as we are enclosed in our bodily framework, we are forced by fate to perform a hard task, for the soul has a heavenly quality and is thrust down from its lofty home and, so to speak, buried in the earth, which is alien to the soul's divine and eternal nature. I believe the purpose of the immortal gods in implanting souls in human bodies was to provide guardians of the earth, who would observe the harmony of heaven and reproduce it in the consistent moderation of their own lives. Such is the speed at which the soul acts, so immense its memory of the past and prescience of the future, so enormous its range of skills and knowledge and discovery, that I am sure a power as vast as this must be immortal; and as the soul is always active and never begins to move, because it is the source of its own movement, it will not even stop moving because it will never desert itself. Further, since the soul is homogeneous and contains no alien or inconsistent element, it cannot be divided and therefore cannot perish. . . .

Moreover, in Xenophon Cyrus the elder as he is dying says this: 'My dear sons, do not suppose that, when I leave you, I shall be nowhere and be nothing. While I was with you, you never saw my soul, but knew from my actions that it existed; so in the future you must believe that it keeps its identity though you see nothing of it. Indeed, the renown of famous men would not continue after their death if their souls were doing nothing to keep their memory alive. I have never believed that souls exist in mortal bodies, but die on leaving them, nor that a soul is senseless when it leaves a senseless body; rather, it achieves wisdom when it is freed from the contamination of the body and becomes pure and unblemished. Further, when death dissolves the human body, it is obvious where everything else goes, as all things return to their place of origin; only the soul is invisible, both when it is present and when it is gone. In fact, as you see, sleep more than anything else resembles death. When we are asleep, our souls give the strongest evidence of their divinity, as, when they are relaxed and free, they frequently foresee the future, which shows in what state they will be when completely free of the shackles of the body. And so,' he says, 'if this is true, honour me as a god, but if the soul is to die with the body, you, with reverence for the gods, who are guardians and controllers of this ordered universe, will I know cherish my memory in love and devotion.' . . .

These are Cyrus' dying words; now, with your leave we will look nearer home [i.e. at Roman examples].

Now that I have run away, I should not like to be called back from the finishing tape to the starting point. What are the advantages of life? Is not man born to toil? Yes, life has advantages: but one can have enough or too much of it. The thought of life does not move me to sorrow, as it has moved many learned men, and I do not regret the life I have led. I have lived in such a way that I do not think I was born in vain, and as I say good-bye to life, I feel that I depart as a guest, not one leaving home; this world is given to us as an inn in which to stay, but not to dwell.

CICERO
(trans. Austin Whitaker)

It Matters Not

It matters not when I am dead
Where this dull clay shall lie,
Nor what the dogmas, creeds and rites
Decree to us who die.
I only know that I shall tread
The paths my dead have trod,
And where the hearts I love have gone,
There shall I find my God.

KENDALL BANNING

Bishop Brent was born in Canada, but worked chiefly in the United States and the Philippines. He was intimately concerned with the ecumenical movement in the Anglican Church. He also served as Chief of Chaplains to the US expeditionary force in Europe, 1917–19.

What is dying? I am standing on the sea shore. A ship sails to the morning breeze and starts for the ocean. She is an object of beauty and I stand watching her till at last she fades on the horizon, and someone at my side says, 'She is gone.' Gone where? Gone from my sight, that is all; she is just as large in the masts, hull and spars as she was when I saw her, and just as able to bear her load of living freight to its destination.

The diminished size and total loss of sight is in me, not in her; and just at the moment when someone at my side says, 'She is gone,' there are others who are watching her coming, and other voices take up a glad shout, 'There she comes' – and that is dying.

BISHOP BRENT

Perhaps a change of mood is welcome. In Mrs Gaskell's 'North and South', Bessy mentions Revelation 7, one of the best-known Christian chapters suggesting what might be awaiting us. (The chapter ends with the words: 'The Lamb . . . shall feed them, and shall lead them unto living fountains of waters; and God shall wipe away all tears from their eyes.') There is a similar but much less well-known passage in the Apocrypha which is included here immediately after the Gaskell extract. The passage was of course written before the birth of Christ, but the clergyman who drew my attention to it commented: 'The more famous Revelation passage seems less Christian by comparison.'

From **North and South**

'I shall have a spring where I'm boun' to, and flowers, and amar-
anths, and shining robes besides . . . If yo'd led the life I have,
and thought at times, "maybe it'll last for fifty or sixty years – it
does wi' some," – and got dizzy and dazed, and sick, as each of
them sixty years seemed to spin about me, and mock me with its
length of hours and minutes, and endless bits o' time – oh, wench!
I tell thee thou'd been glad enough when th' doctor said he feared
thou'd never see another winter.'
   'Why, Bessy, what kind of a life has yours been?'
   'Nought worse than many others', I reckon. Only I fretted
again' it, and they didn't . . . I never knew why folk in the Bible
cared for soft raiment afore. But it must be nice to go dressed as
yo' do. It's different fro' common . . . Sometimes I'm so tired out
I think I cannot enjoy heaven without a piece of rest first. I'm
rather afeard o' going straight there without getting a good sleep
in the grave to set me up . . . Sometimes, when I've thought o'
my life, and the little pleasure I've had in it, I've believed that,
maybe, I was one of those doomed to die by the falling of a star
from heaven . . . One can bear pain and sorrow better if one thinks
it has been prophesied long before for one: somehow, then, it
seems as if my pain was needed for the fulfilment; otherways it
seems all sent for nothing.'
   'Nay, Bessy – think!' said Margaret. 'God does not willingly
afflict. Don't dwell so much on the prophecies, but read the clearer
parts of the Bible.'
   'I dare say it would be wiser; but where would I hear such grand
words of promise – hear tell o' anything so far different fro' this
dreary world, and this town above a', as in Revelations? Many's
the time I've repeated the verses in the seventh chapter to myself,
just for the sound. It's as good as an organ, and as different from
every day, too. No, I cannot give up Revelations. It gives me
more comfort than any other book i' the Bible.'

                                                    ELIZABETH GASKELL

From **The Apocrypha**

I Esdras saw upon the mount Sion a great people, whom I could
not number, and they all praised the Lord with songs.
   And in the midst of them there was a young man of a high

stature, taller than all the rest, and upon every one of their heads he set crowns, and was more exalted: which I marvelled at greatly.

So I asked the angel, and said, Sir, what are these?

He answered and said unto me, These be they that have put off the mortal clothing, and put on the immortal, and have confessed the name of God: now they are crowned, and receive palms.

Then said I unto the angel, What young person is it that crowneth them, and giveth them palms in their hands?

So he answered and said unto me, It is the Son of God, whom they have confessed in the world. Then began I greatly to commend them that stood so stiffly for the name of the Lord.

Then the angel said unto me, Go thy way, and tell my people what manner of things, and how great wonders of the Lord thy God, thou hast seen.

2 ESDRAS 2:42–8

From **Letters to Malcolm**

About the resurrection of the body. I agree with you that the old picture of the soul reassuming the corpse – perhaps blown to bits or long since usefully dissipated through nature – is absurd. Nor is it what St Paul's words imply. And I admit that if you ask what I substitute for this, I have only speculations to offer.

The principle behind these speculations is this. We are not, in this doctrine, concerned with matter as such at all: with waves and atoms and all that. What the soul cries out for is the resurrection of the senses. Even in this life matter would be nothing to us if it were not the source of sensations.

Now we already have some feeble and intermittent power of raising dead sensations from their graves. I mean, of course, memory.

You see the way my thought is moving. But don't run away with the idea that when I speak of the resurrection of the body I mean merely that the blessed dead will have excellent memories of their sensuous experiences on earth. I mean it the other way round: that memory as we now know it is a dim foretaste, a mirage even, of a power which the soul, or rather Christ in the soul (he 'went to prepare a place for us') will exercise hereafter. It need no longer be intermittent. Above all, it need no longer be private to the soul in which it occurs. I can now communicate to you the vanished fields of my boyhood – they are building-estates today – only imperfectly by words. Perhaps the day is coming when I can take you for a walk through them.

At present we tend to think of the soul as somehow 'inside' the body. But the glorified body of the resurrection as I conceive it – the sensuous life raised from its death – will be inside the soul. As God is not in space but space is in God.

I have slipped in 'glorified' almost unawares. But this glorification is not only promised, it is already foreshadowed. The dullest of us knows how memory can transfigure; how often some momentary glimpse of beauty in boyhood is

> a whisper
> Which memory will warehouse as a shout.

Don't talk to me of the 'illusions' of memory. Why should what we see at the moment be more 'real' than what we see from ten years' distance? It is indeed an illusion to believe that the blue hills on the horizon would still look blue if you went to them. But the fact that they are blue five miles away, and the fact that they are green when you are on them, are equally good facts. Traherne's 'orient and immortal wheat' or Wordsworth's landscape 'apparelled in celestial light' may not have been so radiant in the past when it was present as in the remembered past. That is the beginning of the glorification. One day they will be more radiant still. Thus in the sense-bodies of the redeemed the whole New Earth will arise. The same yet not the same as this. It was sown in corruption, it is raised in incorruption.

I dare not omit, though it may be mocked and misunderstood, the extreme example. The strangest discovery of a widower's life is the possibility, sometimes, of recalling with detailed and uninhibited imagination, with tenderness and gratitude, a passage of carnal love, yet with no re-awakening of concupiscence. And when this occurs (it must not be sought) awe comes upon us. It is like seeing Nature itself rising from its grave. What was sown in momentariness is raised in still permanence. What was sown as a becoming rises as being. Sown in subjectivity, it rises in objectivity. The transitory secret of two is now a chord in the ultimate music.

'But this', you protest, 'is no resurrection of the *body*. You have given the dead a sort of dream world and dream bodies. They are not real.' Surely neither less nor more real than those you have always known: you know better than I that the 'real world' of our present experience (coloured, resonant, soft or hard, cool or warm, all corseted by perspective) has no place in the world described by physics or even physiology. Matter enters our experience only by becoming sensation (when we perceive it) or conception (when we understand it). That is, by becoming soul. That element in the soul which it becomes will, in my view, be raised and glorified; the hills and valleys of Heaven will be to those you now experience not as a copy is to an original, nor as a substitute to the genuine article, but as the flower to the root, or the diamond to the coal. It will be eternally true that they originate with matter; let us therefore bless matter. But in entering our soul as alone it can enter – that is, by being perceived and known – matter has turned into soul. . . .

I don't say the resurrection of this body will happen at once. It may well be that this part of us sleeps in death and the intellectual soul is sent to Lenten lands where she fasts in naked spirituality – a ghostlike and imperfectly human condition. I don't imply that an angel is a ghost. But naked spirituality is in accordance with his nature: not, I think, with ours. (A two-legged horse is maimed but not a two-legged man.) Yet from that fact my hope is that we shall return and re-assume the wealth we laid down.

Then the new earth and sky, the same yet not the same as these, will rise in us as we have risen in Christ. And once again, after who knows what aeons of the silence and the dark, the birds will sing out and the waters flow, and lights and shadows move across the hills and the faces of our friends laugh upon us with amazed recognition.

Guesses, of course, only guesses. If they are not true, something better will be. For we know that we shall be made like Him, for we shall see Him as He is.

C. S. LEWIS

The Paradox

Our death implicit in our birth,
We cease, or cannot be;
And know when we are laid in earth
We perish utterly.

And equally the spirit knows
The indomitable sense
Of immortality, which goes
Against all evidence.

See faith alone, whose hand unlocks
All mystery at a touch,
Embrace the awful Paradox
Nor wonder overmuch.

RUTH PITTER

*This passage comes from a sermon given by Lord Ballantrae, Chancellor
of St Andrews University, to students in the university chapel, not long
before he died in 1980.*

Who or What God is I do not pretend to know. I have encountered
in my travels so many different conceptions of Him, ranging from
those of the simplest Christian faith, such as the Karen Baptists of
Burma, to devout animists and pagans from Nigeria to the Pacific
Islands. But that there *is* a God is doubted by few people; and it
does not worry me that many of those few are among those whose
intelligence is rated most highly.

Nor am I worried that we know so little about God; nor by the
question so often asked, as though it were the end to all argument:
'If there *is* a God, why does he allow so much suffering, and
sorrow, and pain?'

It seems to me an impertinence, a piece of arrogance, that at this
earthly stage of our development we should expect to know all
the answers. It so happens that I no longer own a dog, but I have
owned several in my time. Each knew the area around my house:
in fact, they knew it in far more detail than I did; but the world
that they knew was confined to a few miles; they were not
equipped, nor did they aspire, to know more. And as for pain:
what parent is there among us who has not had to inflict pain
upon a beloved child, without being able to explain that in the
long run it is for his or her own good? It may be a minor thing,
like a mere jab against diphtheria; but I am still haunted by the
memory of abandoning my three-year-old son, who was prote-
sting deafeningly and with tears at being left in a hospital to have
his tonsils out. How could I explain to him why we were doing
it to him? I am satisfied to believe that one day we will understand
all this: even such things as early and unexpected and seemingly
undeserved bereavement.

This brings us on to the question of whether or not there is what we call – for want of a better phrase – 'an after-life'. I believe with complete confidence that there is; and in this belief I have never wavered, whether in peace or war. I have already confessed that I make no pretence to knowing Who or What God is; but I am sure that we all owe our existence to something much higher than a passing moment of sexual ecstasy between our parents. I find it impossible to believe that creatures so complex as every one of us is could have been called into being for such a short span as is granted even to those who have the doubtful privilege of living longest. I can no more imagine Death as being final than I can imagine Space ending in a brick wall, or in a sort of celestial knacker's yard.

Nor can I accept the Buddhist idea of Nirvana, where we are all absorbed into one perfected anonymous personality. I believe – and again, this is a belief in which I have never wavered – that we will be reunited with those whom we have loved, and with those who have loved us: as individuals whom we will recognize, and who will recognize us: in happiness, perfected and made whole.

When I was a boy at school, a singularly silly woman was cross-examining my headmaster about the curriculum. She wanted to know why her son was not being taught such things as book-keeping, accountancy, business practices, and the like. He endured her for a while in patience; until at last she asked him point-blank: 'In a word, Dr Alington, what *are* you educating my son for?' And he replied: 'In a word, Madam, for Death.'

There was more in that reply than mere wit. Paradoxically, the one thing that is certain in this Life is Death. If we think that, when it comes, it will clang down before us like a portcullis, or down upon us like a guillotine, then indeed, as St Paul said, 'then is our faith vain'. But it is not only 'wishful thinking' that makes me reject this. All my reasoning compels me to believe that a 'creature' – in the literal sense of that word – so complicated as I am cannot be snuffed out like a candle. Immortality may seem unlikely; but to me anything less is not only unlikely; it is incredible.

Each evening from my home in the hills 300 feet above the village of Ballantrae, I see the sun setting beyond the long peninsula of Kintyre, knowing that it will rise again behind me next morning over the hill of Beneraird. Every autumn as the days grow shorter, I know that the spring will come again with all its welcome signs:

the whaups bubbling away on the hill, the lambs cavorting, and the larches bursting out. These are signs of the faith which is instinctive in all of us; and so is the birth of every new baby.

These 'intimations of immortality', in Wordsworth's felicitous phrase, reassure us with their rhythm and their constancy, and fortify our sure and certain hope of even better things to come.

LORD BALLANTRAE

Rabindranath Tagore, the Hindu poet and philosopher, wrote in English also.

From Sadhana

It fills me with great joy and a high hope for the future of humanity when I realize that there was a time in the remote past when our poet-prophets stood under the lavish sunshine of an Indian sky and greeted the world with the glad recognition of kindred . . . It was not seeing man reflected everywhere in grotesquely exaggerated images, and witnessing the human drama acted on a gigantic scale in nature's arena of flitting lights and shadows. On the contrary, it meant crossing the limiting barriers of an individual, to become more than man, to become one with the All . . . These ancient seers felt in the serene depth of their mind that the same energy, which vibrates and passes into the endless forms of the world, manifests itself in our inner being as consciousness; and there is no break in unity. For these seers there was no gap in their luminous vision of perfection. They never acknowledged even death itself as creating a chasm in the field of reality. They said, *His reflection is death as well as immortality.* They did not recognize any essential opposition between life and death, and they said with absolute assurance, 'It is life that is death'. They saluted with the same serenity of gladness 'life in its aspect of appearing and in its aspect of departure' – *That which is past is hidden in life, and that which is to come.* They knew that mere appearance and disappearance are on the surface like waves on the sea, but life which is permanent knows no decay or diminution.

Everything is sprung from immortal life and is vibrating with life, for life is immense.

RABINDRANATH TAGORE

Some may find great comfort in Donne's words about the togetherness of the living and the dead.

He was but a Heathen that said, If God love a man, He takes him young out of this world; and they were but Heathens, that observed that custome, to put on mourning when their sons were born, and to feast and triumph when they dyed. But thus much we may learne from these Heathens, that if the dead, and we, be not upon one floore, nor under one story, yet we are under one roofe. We think not a friend lost, because he is gone into another roome, nor because he is gone into another Land; And into another world, no man is gone, for that Heaven, which God created, and this world, is all one world. If I had fixt a Son in Court, or married a daughter into a plentiful fortune, I were satisfied for that son and that daughter. Shall I not be so, when the King of Heaven hath taken that son to himselfe, and married himselfe to that daughter, for ever? I spend none of my Faith, I excercise none of my Hope, in this, that I shall have my dead raised to life againe.

This is the faith that sustains me, when I lose by the death of others, or when I suffer by living in misery myselfe. That the dead and we, are now all in one Church, and at the resurrection, shall be all in one Quire.

JOHN DONNE

Alan Paton, perhaps best known for his 'Cry the Beloved Country', wrote 'Kontakion for You Departed' after his young wife Dorrie died. It looks back to their life together and is a tribute to her.

Where are you, my love? And in what condition? That your body has returned to the dust, that I know. But what has happened to you, to your love and your warmth and your courage? Your dust is indestructible, but you, you yourself, were you also indestructible? Did you, you yourself, have no being apart from that body that has returned to the dust?

I write these words with great care. I have no desire to believe something just because I desire to believe it. The Archbishop said,

With the passing of Dorrie the visible fellowship is broken; but death does not put an end to real fellowship; prayer goes on and love continues – from the land of the living, from the joy of Paradise, whence all pain and grief have fled away, where the light of Christ's countenance ever shines.

Was he speaking about Heaven? Are you in Heaven? Are you

reunited there to your first husband, your father and your mother, your much-loved sister Rad, your brother Ray who died as a boy, the one you said I would have liked especially, because we were so like each other? Would your first husband perhaps not be there, because he was not a believer, and would I perhaps go there because I am a believer? This whole speculation is to me so grotesque that I cannot indulge in it. If I wish to touch you again, if I wish again to feel your warm and loving body pressed against mine after long separation, then I can do it only in memory . . .

I believe you died in God's will, and that you are eternal, but of your place and condition I know nothing, and I do not speculate about it . . .

If I am ever in any kind of sense of the word to *know* you again, there will be no jealousies and angers and arrogances and impatiences, but only joy. And sorrow and pain shall be no more, neither sighing, but life everlasting.

And if such things are never to be, then I give thanks this day for what is and has been. And I can doubly give thanks, for during the writing of these words, I have come out of the valley of darkness.

Did you intercede for me?

ALAN PATON

For those who profess no religion, here is one of the great Victorian freethinkers tackling what is, with double meaning, the eternal question.

> O may I join the choir invisible
> Of those immortal dead who live again
> In minds made better by their presence: live
> In pulses stirred to generosity,
> In deeds of daring rectitude, in scorn
> For miserable aims that end with self,
> In thoughts sublime that pierce the night like stars,
> And with their mild persistence urge man's search
> To vaster issues . . .
>   This is the life to come,
> Which martyred men have made more glorious
> For us who strive to follow. May I reach
> That purest heaven, be to other souls
> The cup of strength in some great agony,
> Enkindle generous ardour, feed pure love,

Beget the smiles that have no cruelty –
Be the sweet presence of a good diffused,
And in diffusion ever more intense.
So shall I join the choir invisible
Whose music is the gladness of the world.

GEORGE ELIOT

*This passage by William Penn the Quaker seems not in the least archaic,
although it was written in the seventeenth century.*

Death being the way and condition of life, we cannot love to live
if we cannot bear to die. I have often wondered at the unaccount-
ableness of man in this, among other things; that tho' he loves
changes so well, he should care so little to hear or think of his last,
great and best change too, if he pleases. The truest end of Life, is,
to know the Life that never ends. He that lives to live ever, never
fears dying. Nor can the Means be terrible to him that heartily
believes the End. For tho' Death be a Dark Passage, it leads to
Immortality, and that's Recompense enough for suffering of it.

They that loved *beyond the World* cannot be separated by it
[death].

Death cannot kill what never dies. Nor can Spirits ever be
divided that love and live in the same Divine Principle; the *Root*
and *Record* of their friendship.

If Absence be not Death, neither is theirs. Death is but the
Crossing the World, as friends do the Seas; They live in one another
still.

For they must needs be present, that love and live in that which
is *Omnipresent*.

In this Divine Glass they see Face to Face; and their converse is
Free as well as Pure.

This is the comfort of Friends, that though they may be said to
Die, yet their Friendship and Society are, in the best Sense, ever
present, because *Immortal*.

WILLIAM PENN

The seventeenth-century lines below are occasionally sung as a hymn:

He wants not friends that hath thy love,
And may converse and walk with thee,
And with thy saints here and above,
With whom for ever I must be.

In the blest fellowship of saints
Is wisdom, safety and delight;
And when my heart declines and faints,
It's raisèd by their heat and light.

As for my friends, they are not lost:
The several vessels of thy fleet,
Though parted now, by tempests tost
Shall safely in the haven meet.

Still we are centred all in thee,
Members, though distant, of one Head;
In the same family we be,
By the same faith and spirit led.

Before thy throne we daily meet
As joint-petitioners to thee;
In spirit we each other greet,
And shall again each other see.

The heavenly hosts, world without end,
Shall be my company above;
And thou, my best and surest friend,
Who shall divide me from thy love?

                                    RICHARD BAXTER

Joyce Grenfell writes to a dear friend.

Believing as I do that man is spiritual here and now *wherever* he may seem to be, I have no doubts that [F] is simply continuing in the continuity of life; and, that is, in the spiritual realm where she has always essentially been. We think we love someone for their looks; their walk maybe; tone of voice, touch – but when you analyse it it is really for their qualities – their warmth, their humour, their intelligence, kindness, etc. These things are spiritual qualities and are recognisable only by the spiritual in us. This, to me, is proof of spirituality. We may think it's the shape of a person's nose or the way the eyes light up or whatever it is, but in fact it is the *impression* these things have on us and this is not physical or material, is it? So, although the sense of loss is brutal and a shock – when you can look at it and think of it and feel the very real gratitude you have for having known and loved someone, then I think a sense of *real* reality takes over and one comes to the reasonable conclusion that spirituality is a reality; a continuing reality of all-good. . .

I believe the way to peace is not to mourn, but to free her in your mind and heart and realise she is always whole, always real because she is spiritual – *and so are you.*

We don't become spiritual *when* we die. We have always been spiritual and that, as I see it, is what life is for – to discover and rejoice in this. It leads into harmonious living *now.* It reveals what is actually *real* and *durable.*

JOYCE GRENFELL

These lines are supposed to have been written by Sir Walter Raleigh, a few hours before he was executed. After his death they were said to have been found between two pages of his bible.

> Even such is Time, which takes in trust
>   Our youth, our joys, and all we have,
> And pays us but with age and dust:
>   Who in the dark and silent grave,
> When we have wandered all our ways
>   Shuts up the story of our days:
> And from which earth and grave and dust,
>   The Lord shall raise me up, I trust.

SIR WALTER RALEIGH

Archbishop Fénelon played a significant part in French politics in the late seventeenth century, but his letters of spiritual counsel have been of lasting value.

In our eyes, the dead are as if they had gone away for a few years, or even months. We apparently lose them, and this should free our grasp on the world, where everything must eventually be lost. We shall be beckoned to the world beyond, where all shall be found once more.

ARCHBISHOP FÉNELON
(trans. Antony Whitaker)

The source of this verse is not known, though it is believed to be American.

I have seen death too often to believe in death.
It is not an ending – but a withdrawal.
As one who finishes a long journey,
    Stills the motor,
    Turns off the lights,
    Steps from his car,
And walks up the path
To the home that awaits him.

        BLANDING

Henry Scott Holland (1847–1918) was a man of independent views, always keen to have Christian ideas made relevant to human problems. He wrote the hymn 'Judge eternal, throned in splendour'.

Death is nothing at all . . . I have only slipped away into the next room. I am I and you are you. Whatever we were to each other that we are still. Call me by my old familiar name, speak to me in the easy way which you always used. Put no difference in your tone; wear no forced air of solemnity or sorrow. Laugh as we always laughed at the little jokes we enjoyed together. Play, smile, think of me, pray for me. Let my name be ever the household word that it always was. Let it be spoken without effort, without the ghost of a shadow on it. Life means all that it ever meant. It is the same as it ever was; there is absolutely unbroken continuity. Why should I be out of mind because I am out of sight? I am waiting for you for an interval, somewhere very near, just around the corner. All is well.

        HENRY SCOTT HOLLAND

6

The seasons of the heart

. . . in spite of all,
Some shape of beauty moves away the pall
From our dark spirits.

JOHN KEATS, 'ENDYMION', BOOK I

This chapter is about patterns – patterns of death and life, sorrow and joy, sunset and sunrise, winter and spring, ends and beginnings.

It touches on the more profound questions as to whether humans have a place, superior or humble, in the natural order of things, or whether material reality is the work of love, and especially of the love of God.

A bereaved woman described the snowdrops she was sent as 'a point of hope'. Again and again natural beauty brings symbols: symbols of a new stage, a step forward, or symbols for the future. Again and again, too, the days and seasons reflect our feelings.

It does undoubtedly calm us to reflect on the awesome age and grandeur of mountains, the limpid tranquillity of lakes and streams, huge waves curling over rocks and sending up high plumes of spray, or the palest green velvety leaves of beechwoods, shot through with sunlight – even if the result is what Hesse calls 'sorrow-steeped enchantment'.

More importantly, we might gain (either slowly, or dramatically as did Winifred Holtby in the worst circumstances – see page 90) a sense that we are at home in the universe, a sense of tranquillity within the accustomed patterns, a tranquillity that might gradually take away the fear and alarm from our lives.

From **Death and the Family**

Does it comfort the adult bereaved to know that their dead help to grow something, that something remains as seed in the ground, in the universe, in other people, in the bereaved himself? Do adults – like children – have a heightened awareness of new life, of

creation, when they have to face death? Does it comfort the
bereaved to know that death and birth are part of the continuing
cycle of life – transitory and eternal?

There is no growth without pain and conflict: there is no loss
which cannot lead to gain. Although this interconnection is what
life is all about, it is difficult for the newly bereaved to accept.
Only slowly may he, who has been in touch with death through
the loss of a significant person, regain touch with life. A life which
may bring new growth through the acceptance of death and pain
and loss, and thus become truly a new life, a rebirth.

LILY PINCUS

*These extracts from Wordsworth's 'Tintern Abbey' are well known but
perhaps not quite as familiar to us as some others, like the line 'the still,
sad music of humanity', or the great climax of the poem, the poet's credo
of 'something far more deeply interfused, whose dwelling is the light of
setting suns'.*

*These extracts are included here partly to suggest that you find the
poem and read it all again – or for the first time. There are many insights
which bereaved people might find valuable, expressed in simple language
without obscurity.*

These beauteous forms,
Through a long absence, have not been to
me
As is a landscape to a blind man's eye:
But oft, in lonely rooms, and 'mid the din
Of towns and cities, I have owed to them,
In hours of weariness, sensations sweet,
Felt in the blood, and felt along the heart;
And passing even into my purer mind,
With tranquil restoration . . .

Nor less, I trust,
To them I may have owed another gift,
Of aspect more sublime; that blessed mood,
In which the burthen of the mystery,
In which the heavy and the weary weight
Of all this unintelligible world,
Is lightened: that serene and blessed mood,
In which the affections gently lead us on,
Until, the breath of this corporeal frame

And even the motion of our human blood
Almost suspended, we are laid asleep
In body, and become a living soul:
While with an eye made quiet by the
    power
Of harmony, and the deep power of joy,
We see into the life of things . . .

And now, with gleams of half-extinguished thought,
With many recognitions dim and faint,
And somewhat of a sad perplexity,
The picture of the mind revives again:
While here I stand, not only with the sense
Of present pleasure, but with pleasing
    thoughts
That in this moment there is life and food
For future years . . .

                              WILLIAM WORDSWORTH

From **A Thousand-Mile Walk to the Gulf**

Let children walk with Nature, let them see the beautiful blendings
and communions of death and life, their joyous inseparable unity,
and they will learn that death is stingless indeed, and as beautiful
as life, and that the grave has no victory, for it never fights.

                                      JOHN MUIR

*Below, in religious terms, Martin Israel describes the incomplete experi-
ences of mysticism that he believes many of us can find.*
   *This extract, and those on pages 96, 126 and 131, come from his
supportive book 'Living Alone', where the subject is approached in both
depth and width, within a Christian context.*

The unitive experience occurs as a milestone on the spiritual path.
Far from being the end of the journey, it is a confirmation by
God's grace that all one has stored in one's faith is a living reality.
It comes like the wind, blowing as it will, so that no one can tell
where it comes from or where it is to go. This is the way of the
Holy Spirit. I do not believe that anyone who is on the path of
discipleship is left without an experience of union of God with the
created universe, but there are all grades from the fully manifested

experience which is known to the great mystics of the race to the fleeting peak experiences that lighten the worldly darkness of the humble aspirant. It is not the intensity of the experience that determines its validity, but rather the effect it has on the future life of the disciple.

MARTIN ISRAEL

Here is a secular example of a possible mystical experience which brought an immense feeling of oneness with the universe, and strong resolution for the future, however bleak it seemed.

The busy creative life and early death of the writer Winifred Holtby is told by her friend Vera Brittain in 'Testament of Friendship'.

On one of the coldest mornings of that spring, after she had learnt from a London specialist that she might not have more than two years to live, she went for a walk past Clare Leighton's cottage to a farm further up the hill. She felt tired and dejected; her mind, still vigorously alive in her slow, impaired body, rebelled bitterly against her fate. Why, she wondered, should she, at thirty-three, not yet in the fullness of her developing powers, be singled out for this cruel unforeseen blow? She knew, for the constant demands of her friends had made it clear to her, that her life was infinitely valuable to others. She thought of all the half-dead people who 'put in time', as though time were not the greatest gift in the universe, while she, who could use it so superbly, was soon to be deprived of it for ever; and she felt that her mind could hardly contain the rising anguish of that realization.

Just then she found herself standing by a trough outside the farmyard; the water in it was frozen and a number of young lambs were struggling beside it vainly trying to drink. She broke the ice for them with her stick, and as she did so she heard a voice within her saying: 'Having nothing, yet possessing all things.' It was so distinct that she looked round, startled, but she was alone with the lambs on the top of the hill. Suddenly, in a flash, the grief, the bitterness, the sense of frustration disappeared; all desire to possess power and glory for herself vanished away, and never came back. She walked down the hill with the exhilaration which, says Storm Jameson in *Civil Journey*, 'springs from the sense of having lost everything. It is a feeling like no other, a curious form of spiritual intoxication, perhaps not repeatable.'

Winifred never told me of this incident nor of the sentence of death passed upon her, until June 1935, when she had only three months to live. By that time she thought – or, as I now suspect, allowed me to believe that she thought – that she had outwitted the doctors. The moment of 'conversion' on the hill at Monks Risborough, she said with tears in her eyes, was the supreme spiritual experience of her life. She always associated it afterwards with the words of Bernard Bosanquet on Salvation:

'And now we are saved absolutely, we need not say from what, we are at home in the universe, and, in principle and in the main, feeble and timid creatures as we are, there is nothing anywhere within the world or without it that can make us afraid.'

VERA BRITTAIN

Peace in the Welsh Hills

Here, where the earth is green, where heaven is true
Opening the windows, touched with earliest dawn,
In the first frost of cool September days,
Chrysanthemum weather, presaging great birth,
Who in his heart could murmur or complain:
'The light we look for is not in this land?'
That light is present and that distant time
Is always here, continually redeemed.

VERNON WATKINS

The next two poems, and those on pages 120 and 123, were written by Margaret Torrie, who founded Cruse in 1959.

The Question

Where is the song now
    when all is silent
    and the grey clouds
    mock the sun
    and the husk is empty and dry?
Where is the bright joy
    when the bird on the wing
    is snared
    and ice settles on the water?

How may I travel
the winter solstice
when the blood slows
and the heart quivers
and is silent?
Will you in the shroud
and the dead leaf
show me a new beginning
the kingdom and the crown
in the darkness?

MARGARET TORRIE

Prayer to the Alchemist

I pray you
take this weeping heart
and all the broken thing
that lies within Your hand
Distil the agony
until
from all its hurt
a single drop of sweetness
may remain
changing the substance
of this death in earth
to make all new –
a rising sap
to bring the transformation
of the spring

MARGARET TORRIE

From In Memoriam

Now fades the last long streak of snow,
  Now burgeons every maze of quick
  About the flowering squares, and thick
By ashen roots the violets blow.

Now rings the woodland loud and long.
  The distance takes a lovelier hue,
  And drown'd in yonder living blue
The lark becomes a sightless song.

Now dance the lights on lawn and lea,
  The flocks are whiter down the vale,
  And milkier every milky sail
On winding stream or distant sea;

Where now the seamew pipes, or dives
  In yonder greening gleam, and fly
  The happy birds, that change their sky
To build and brood; that live their lives

From land to land; and in my breast
  Spring wakens too; and my regret
  Becomes an April violet,
And buds and blossoms like the rest.

Love is and was my Lord and King,
  And in his presence I attend
  To hear the tidings of my friend,
Which every hour his courtiers bring.

Love is and was my King and Lord,
  And will be, tho' as yet I keep
  Within his court on earth, and sleep
Encompass'd by his faithful guard,

And hear at times a sentinel
  Who moves about from place to place,
  And whispers to the worlds of space,
In the deep night, that all is well.

ALFRED, LORD TENNYSON

The link between Easter and spring

It is because of the link with the changing moon that there has
been so little success for efforts to give Easter a fixed date.
   The lunar connection matters to believers in at least two ways.
It is part of the demonstration that the first Easter, although the
year and therefore the precise calendar date are not certainly
known, did happen at a specific moment in time. More than that,

it is a reminder that the holding of the supreme Christian festival
is governed not by the cosy conveniences of school terms and
public holidays but by the movement of celestial influences free of
human control. It is a witness to the place in human life of the
transcendent.

That said, there is no question that Easter has extra effect when
the moving moon allows it to fall late. The greening of the trees
. . . does help. Most Christian theologians are made uneasy by a
parallel between Easter and spring. You can find the parallel in
hymns, the plain man's theology tutors, from the sixth century to
the twentieth; but stricter theologians want a line drawn between
a once-for-all divine intervention and a once-a-year renewal of the
earth.

Nevertheless, the greening of the trees is an eloquent allegorical
expression of some of the claims that Easter makes: that nothing
is hopeless; that creation is forgiving and resourceful; that the worst
of us, the worst of times, is constantly given a new chance; that
(in Tennyson's diffident dream) 'good shall fall, At last – far off –
at last, to all, And every winter change to spring.'

JOHN WHALE

From **The Flower**

How fresh, O Lord, how sweet and clean
Are thy returns! Even as the flowers in spring;
To which, besides their own demean,
The late-past frosts tributes of pleasure bring.
Grief melts away
Like snow in May,
As if there were no such cold thing.

Who would have thought my shrivell'd heart
Could have recover'd greenness? It was gone
Quite under ground; as flowers depart
To see their Mother-root, when they have blown;
Where they together
All the hard weather,
Dead to the world, keep house unknown. . . .

And now in age I bud again,
After so many deaths I live and write;
I once more smell the dew and rain,
And relish versing: O my only light,
    It cannot be
    That I am he,
On whom thy tempests fell all night.

GEORGE HERBERT

From **Reflections**

When we return from . . . happiness to self-awareness and to our
knowledge of life's misery, our joy returns to sadness, the world
shows us not its radiant sky but the blackness underneath, and
then beauty and art make us sad. But they remain beautiful, they
remain divine, and this is true of the fugue, the painting, the gull's
tail feathers, the oil spot, and of far lesser things.

And even though the joy of forgetting oneself and the world
lasts only for brief moments, the sorrow-steeped enchantment that
rises from the miracle of beauty can endure for hours, for a lifetime.

HERMANN HESSE

*The first anniversary is, for many of you, the last significant ordeal of
the period of bereavement, and you dread it. Some who pass through it
testify that the actual day is not so bad as the dreading beforehand. Others
had not expected its impact would be so great, and it jumps on them
unawares. Many find the day's passing brings a sense of release; others
hope that the anniversary might work some magic, and it doesn't.*

*You may find that you do something that day which seems afterwards
to have been symbolic. You might like to climb a hill. Whatever your
religious beliefs, you might care to spend twenty minutes in one of our
very old churches or cathedrals.*

*I was once alone with my thoughts in the most ancient part of Winchester
Cathedral, when a voluntary guide came in with a group of visitors. In
a far-carrying voice she explained: 'This chapel is kept so that members
of the public can have a quiet place for their thoughts and prayers.' My
thoughts became lost, distracted, and were replaced with silent laughter at
the irony. The person who had died, who was in my thoughts, would
have laughed too. We seemed to share it. In a roundabout way the guide
did us a service.*

Did you know, you who are bereaved, that your close friends and relatives are specially carrying you in their thoughts or prayers as you approach the first anniversary, and on the day itself? They may not say anything to you, and may be diffident about sending a card or flowers, but they are remembering the pain you bore a year ago, and have borne ever since – this week more sharply again. You are held warmly in their caring thoughts.

Martin Israel mentions the first anniversary in 'Living Alone'.

While one must leave the dead to bury their dead as one moves onwards into the present moment with awareness and resolution, it is also important not to suppress one's grief, especially during the first months after the death of a loved one. The first anniversary is a particularly painful period, and the release of pent-up emotions associated with the reawakening of precious memories must not be inhibited. The sacrament of the present moment includes not only the outer events of life that one confronts moment by moment, but also the inner psychic life that impinges itself on one's awareness continually. Beautiful scenery, for instance, not only evokes an intense aesthetic response but may also recall a past rapture with someone who is now dead or perhaps has moved away to another part of the world. The juxtaposition of these two emotional impulses has the effect of lifting one's consciousness to a sublime grasp of reality in which the transience of physical beauty is aligned with the deeper meaning of eternal life. That which is beautiful and noble outlasts its physical form and remains an inspiration to all who subsequently pass on that road of life. When we attend to the present moment and give our life to the passing scene, we add our unique flavour to that moment and that scene so that both the world and ourselves are translated to a new place of bliss. It is in a passing shaft of heightened awareness, such as may follow a sensitive appreciation of the transience of all worldly beauty, that one may be transported to the realm of mystical union and see the eternity that underlies all earthly creation. Then one knows that death is not the end of life but rather its moment of transfiguration to a more spiritual dimension of reality.

MARTIN ISRAEL

From **The Face of the Deep**

> Safe where I cannot lie yet,
>   Safe where I hope to lie too
> Safe from the fume and the fret;
>   You, and you,
> Whom I never forget.
>
> Safe from the frost and the snow,
>   Safe from the storm and the sun,
> Safe where the seeds wait to grow
>   One by one
> And to come back in blow.

CHRISTINA ROSSETTI

The old pattern and the new

We are one people, one community and the death of one is the concern of all. In the face of death man can achieve grandeur, but if he turns his back on death he remains a child, clinging to a land of make-believe. For death is not the ending of the pattern of life's unwinding, but a necessary interruption. Through the painful work of grieving we rediscover the past and weave it afresh into a new reality.

Our aim cannot be to cancel out the past, to try to forget, but to ensure that the strength and meaning which gave beauty to the old pattern is remembered and reinterpreted in the pattern now emerging. Every man must die but the world is permanently changed by each man's existence. At the point of death we meet the forces of social evolution. We may back away in fear, refuse the chance to change, drown our pain in drugs or alcohol or meaningless activity, or we may accept the pains of grief and begin the long struggle to rediscover meaning in a life whose meanings can no longer be taken for granted. There is no easy way through the long valley but we have faith in the ability of each one to find his own way, given time and the encouragement of the rest of us.

COLIN MURRAY PARKES

From Auguries of Innocence

> Man was made for joy and woe:
> And when this we rightly know
> Thro' the world we safely go.
> Joy and woe are woven fine.
> A clothing for the soul divine;
> Under every grief and pine
> Runs a joy with silken twine.

WILLIAM BLAKE

From A Dialogue of Comfort against Tribulation

There is time of weeping and there is time of laughing. But as you see, he setteth the weeping time before, for that is the time of this wretched world and the laughing time shall come after in heaven. There is also a time of sowing, and a time of reaping too. Now must we in this world sow, that we may in the other world reap: and in this short sowing time of this weeping world, must we water our seed with the showers of our tears, and then shall we have in heaven a merry laughing harvest for ever.

SIR THOMAS MORE

The Healing Spring

> Patiently the earth's wounds close,
> The womb heals of its sons
> As bark over a torn branch grows
>
> That we were ever one, my blood
> Obedient to the spring, forgets,
> And growth obliterates the past
> That lies within my heart like death
>
> Oh Love forgive the happiness
> That overgrows and seals my grief.

KATHLEEN RAINE

Remembrance Day

Grieve not for these our dead. The evening star
By her own loveliness assurance gives
That beauty in a darkened world still lives;
So they to us their own sweet sureties are
That goodness still outshines the shades of war.
God is not mocked; his mercy still contrives
Peace for the bleeding flesh, the tired soul shrives
Pronouncing tranquil judgement from afar.
And these were his beloved; have no fear
For them, as, if in hardened hearts like ours
Love sprang unbidden for them, like the flowers
In those their English meadows, yet more dear
Must they remain to him whose gentle tear
Fell for this friend beneath proud Herod's Towers.

QUINTIN HOGG

From Annals of a Quiet Neighbourhood

The sun . . . burst his cloudy bands, and blazed out as if he had
just risen from the dead, instead of being just about to sink into
the grave. Do not tell me that my figure is untrue, for that the
sun never sinks into the grave, else I will retort that it is just as
true of the sun as of a man; for that no man sinks into the grave.
He only disappears. Life is a constant sunrise, which death cannot
interrupt, any more than the night can swallow up the sun.

GEORGE MACDONALD

7

Love than death itself more strong

True love is a durable fire
In the mind ever burning.
Never sick, never old, never dead,
From itself never turning.

SIR WALTER RALEIGH

Several writers have commented that grief is the price we have to pay for love. It does not, however, seem to be true that the greater the love, the greater the grief.

Other factors come into play too. If you have already begun to accept the idea of your own eventual death, you may have gone a little way towards accepting that of a partner or close relative. If you are the kind of person who accepts change quite easily, that again may help a little. If your relationship was good, there may be less guilt and anger to work through later. Someone who is left after a stormy or ambivalent relationship may encounter more anguish than one of a settled pair.

You do not have to prove your love by extending or intensifying your grief. Not one in a thousand will be like Queen Victoria, grieving interminably, trying vainly to preserve some links with the dead Albert. For everyone there is a way through and out, even if a few need some help to find it.

Eventually, instead of memories being an intense form of torture, they gradually cease to wound, and some of them even become quietly pleasing and warm.

Eventually, too, in a remarkable way the dead person seems to have become part of yourself. Some of their opinions, skills, insights and values are intermingled with your own, and in this way they have left the strongest legacy.

From Loss and Change

A sense of continuity can, then, only be restored by detaching the familiar meanings of life from the relationship in which they were embodied, and re-establishing them independently of it. This is what happens in the working through of grief. At first, a widow cannot separate her purposes and understanding from the husband who figured so centrally in them: she has to revive the relationship, to continue it by symbols and make-believe, in order to feel alive. But as time goes by, she begins to reformulate life in terms which assimilate the fact of his death. She makes a gradual transition from talking to him 'as if he were sitting in the chair beside me', to thinking what he would have said and done, and from there to planning her own and her children's future in terms of what he would have wished until finally the wishes become her own, and she no longer consciously refers them to him. So, too, she recasts her relationship to her children, becoming mother and father to them, incorporating her husband's part in their upbringing as an aspect of herself. In the course of this process she will probably change, in personality, in patterns of behaviour, in what she expects from life. But the change will be gradual enough to sustain a continuity of meaning.

Thus grief is mastered, not by ceasing to care for the dead, but by abstracting what was fundamentally important in the relationship and rehabilitating it. A widow has to give up her husband without giving up all that he meant to her, and this task of extricating the essential meaning of the past and reinterpreting it to fit a very different future, seems to proceed by tentative approximations, momentarily comforting but at first unstable. For a while she may not be able to conceive any meanings in her life except those which are backward-looking and memorial, too tragic to sustain any future. In time, if all goes well, she will begin to formulate a sense of her widowhood which neither rejects nor mummifies the past, but continues the same fundamental purposes.

Until then, she will often be overwhelmed by feelings of disintegration.

PETER MARRIS

To Ausonius

I, through all chances that are given to mortals,
    And through all fates that be,
So long as this close prison shall contain me,
    Yea, though a world shall sunder me and thee,

Thee shall I hold, in every fibre woven,
    Not with dumb lips, nor with averted face
Shall I behold thee, in my mind embrace thee,
    Instant and present, thou, in every place.

Yea, when the prison of this flesh is broken,
    And from the earth I shall have gone my way,
Whereso'er in the wide universe I stay me,
    There shall I bear thee, as I do to-day.

Think not the end, that from my body frees me,
    Breaks and unshackles from my love to thee;
Triumphs the soul above its house in ruin,
    Deathless, begot of immortality.

Still must she keep her senses and affections,
    Hold them as dear as life itself to be.
Could she choose death, then might she choose forgetting:
    Living, remembering, to eternity.

PAULINUS OF NOLA
(trans. Helen Waddell)

From **Testament of Youth**

On April 23rd – it was Easter Sunday, and exactly four months after Roland's death – I went to St Paul's Cathedral for the morning service, and sat in a side aisle beneath G. F. Watt's picture of Hagar in the Desert. Her Gethsemane, I thought, had been even darker than that of the Man of Sorrows, who after all knew – or believed – that He was God; she was merely a human being without omnipotence, and a woman too, at the mercy, as were all women today, of an agonizing, ruthless fate which it seemed she could do nothing to restrain. 'Watchman, will the night soon pass?' ran the inscription under the painting, and I wondered how many women in the Cathedral that morning, numbed and bewildered by blow after blow, were asking the self-same question.

Will the night soon pass? Will it ever pass? How much longer can I endure it? What will help me to endure it, if endured it must be?

In a Regent Street tea-shop after the service had ended, I sat over one of the innumerable cups of coffee that we drank during the War in order to get a few moments of privacy, and endeavoured, as earnestly as though humanity itself had entrusted me with the solution of its problems, to discover what was left that would help. In the small notebook that I always carried with me, I scribbled down some of the conclusions at which, in those weeks of wrestling with unseen enemies, I seemed to have arrived.

I know that, come what may, our love will henceforth always be the ruling factor in my life. He is to me the embodiment of that ideal of heroism – that 'Heroism in the Abstract' – for which he lived and died, and for which I will strive to live, and if need be, die also.

If people say to me, 'Why do you do this? It is not necessary, your duty need not take you thus far', I can only answer that in one way heroism is always unnecessary, in so far as it always lies outside the scope of one's limited, stereotyped duty. I do not know with how much or how little courage I should face dangers and perils if they came to me – I am less blindly confident than I once was, for I have been learning a truer estimate of myself, my failings and limitations, in these dark days. I have learnt to hope that if there be a Judgement Day of some kind, God will not see us with our own eyes, nor judge us as we judge ourselves.

But perhaps – and this is my anchor in the present deep waters – self-knowledge is a surer foundation than self-exaltation, and having reached down to it, the ground which nothing can cut away from under my feet, I may achieve more than in the old days. Perhaps one can never rise to the heights until one has gone right down into the depths – such depths as I have known of late.

Perhaps now I shall one day rise, and be worthy of him who in his life both in peace and in war and in his death on the fields of France has shown me 'the way more plain'. At any rate, if ever I do face danger and suffering with some measure of his heroism, it will be because I have learnt through him that love is supreme, that love is stronger than death and the fear of death.

VERA BRITTAIN

From **The Narrow Sea**

> With you for mast, and sail, and flag
> And anchor never known to drag
> Death's narrow but oppressive sea
> Looks not unnavigable to me.

ROBERT GRAVES

*Here is another short passage from 'Death and the Family' where Lily
Pincus describes what happens in grief, in the most lucid terms.*

This process of internalizing the dead, taking the deceased into
oneself and containing him so that he becomes part of one's inner
self, is the most important task in mourning. It does not happen
immediately; for a varying span of time the bereaved is still in
touch with the external presence of the lost person. Once the task
of internalizing has been achieved, the dependence on the external
presence diminishes and the bereaved becomes able to draw on
memories, happy or unhappy, and to share these with others,
making it possible to talk, think, or feel about the dead person.

LILY PINCUS

*This poem is much loved, and often included in anthologies, but we are
seldom told any factual details about it.*

*Heraclitus was a Greek philosopher, living around 500 BC. He wrote
a great work called 'On Nature', whose main theme was that everything
is in a state of eternal flux but ultimately derives from fire. The English
poem is a Victorian translation of an epigram regretting Heraclitus' death,
written by Callimachus, the poet who had a famous school at Alexandria
and was chief librarian of the incomparable library there.*

*There is an aphorism of Heraclitus' that I like very much: 'You cannot
step twice into the same river, for other waters are continually flowing
in.'*

They told me, Heraclitus, they told me you were dead,
They brought me bitter news to hear and bitter tears to shed.
I wept as I remember'd how often you and I
Had tired the sun with talking and sent him down the sky.

And now that thou art lying, my dear old Carian guest,
A handful of grey ashes, long, long ago at rest,
Still are thy pleasant voices, thy nightingales, awake;
For Death, he taketh all away, but them he cannot take.

WILLIAM CORY

Here is another passage from C. S. Lewis's 'A Grief Observed', which shows the beginning of some kind of resolution of his grief. How vividly he expresses his surprising, new feelings.

Something quite unexpected has happened. It came this morning early. For various reasons, not in themselves at all mysterious, my heart was lighter than it had been for many weeks. For one thing, I suppose I am recovering physically from a good deal of mere exhaustion. And I'd had a very tiring but very healthy twelve hours the day before, and a sounder night's sleep; and after ten days of low-hung grey skies and motionless warm dampness, the sun was shining and there was a light breeze. And suddenly at the very moment when, so far, I mourned H. least, I remembered her best. Indeed it was something (almost) better than memory; an instantaneous, unanswerable impression. To say it was like a meeting would be going too far. Yet there was that in it which tempts one to use those words. It was as if the lifting of the sorrow removed a barrier.

Why has no one told me these things? How easily I might have misjudged another man in the same situation. I might have said, 'He's got over it. He's forgotten his wife', when the truth was, 'He remembers her better *because* he has partly got over it.'

Looking back, I see that only a very little time ago I was greatly concerned about my memory of H. and how false it might become. For some reason – the merciful good sense of God is the only one I can think of – I have stopped bothering about that. And the remarkable thing is that since I stopped bothering about it, she seems to meet me everywhere. *Meet* is far too strong a word. I don't mean anything remotely like an apparition or a voice. I don't mean even any strikingly emotional experience at any particular moment. Rather, a sort of unobtrusive but massive sense that she is, just as much as ever, a fact to be taken into account.

C. S. LEWIS

An elderly woman left, on a slip of paper, the italicized lines from this poem, with instructions that they should be read at her funeral. They were, but no one knew the source. Eventually the lines were printed in the Cruse monthly newsletter, which goes to nearly 10,000 members, asking whether any reader could tell us. Just one person replied, enclosing the complete text and the author's name. Since then, many people have written to ask for the full text, so we include it here.

Adieu and Au Revoir

As you love me, let there be
No mourning when I go –
No tearful eyes, no hopeless sighs,
No woe, nor even sadness.
Indeed, I would not have you sad,
For I myself shall be full glad
With the high triumphant gladness
Of a soul made free
Of God's sweet liberty.
No windows darkened, for my own
Will be flung wide, as ne'er before,
To catch the radiant in-pour
Of Love that shall in full atone
For all the ills that I have done.
No voices hushed; my own, full-flushed
With an immortal hope, will rise
In ecstasies of new-born bliss
And joyful melodies.
Rather, of your sweet courtesy
Rejoice with me
At my soul's loosing from captivity.
Wish me 'Bon Voyage' as you do a friend
Whose joyous visit finds its happy end
And bid me both 'Adieu' and 'Au revoir'
Since, though I come no more
I shall be waiting there to greet you
At His door.

And, as the feet of the bearers tread
The ways I trod,
Think not of me as dead, but rather –
Happy, thrice happy, he whose course is sped
He has gone home – to God,
His Father.

JOHN OXENHAM

Here is another passage from the essay on widowhood in Daphne du Maurier's 'The Rebecca Notebook'.

I remember on our wedding day, in July 1932, the good priest who married us drawing a comparison between the little boat in which we were to set forth on our honeymoon and marriage itself. 'You will embark', he said, 'on a fair sea, and at times there will be fair weather, but not always. You will meet storms and overcome them. You will take it in turns to steer your boat through fair weather and foul. Never lose courage. Safe harbour awaits you both in the end.'

Today I remember this advice with gratitude. Even if I must, of necessity, steer my boat alone, I shall not, so I trust, lose my bearings but, because of all I have learnt through the past three-and-thirty years, with my fellow helmsman at my side, come eventually to my journey's end.

As the months pass and the seasons change, something of tranquillity descends, and although the well-remembered footstep will not sound again, nor the voice call from the room beyond, there seems to be about one in the air an atmosphere of love, a living presence. I say this in no haunting sense, ghosts and phantoms are far from my mind. It is as though one shared, in some indefinable manner, the freedom and the peace, even at times the joy, of another world where there is no more pain. It is not a question of faith or of belief. It is not necessary to be a follower of any religious doctrine to become aware of what I mean. It is not the prerogative of the devout. The feeling is simply there, pervading all thought, all action. When Christ the healer said, 'Blessed are they that mourn, for they shall be comforted,' he must have meant just this.

Later, if you go away, if you travel, even if you decide to make your home elsewhere, the spirit of tenderness, of love, will not desert you. You will find that it has become part of you, rising from within yourself; and because of it you are no longer fearful of loneliness, of the dark, because death, the last enemy, has been overcome.

DAPHNE DU MAURIER

From Joyce: by Herself and Her Friends

If I should go before the rest of you,
Break not a flower nor inscribe a stone.
Nor when I'm gone speak in a Sunday voice,
But be the usual selves that I have known.
Weep if you must,
Parting is hell,
But life goes on,
So sing as well.

JOYCE GRENFELL

One of the major adjustments we must make, when someone close to us dies, is to find another focus for our love. Understandably, in the early months, many widowed people consider consulting marriage bureaux and introduction agencies. But most are really looking for the person they have lost, who is irreplaceable of course. It is only possible to seek a different person, another focus, and this can only happen successfully when the grief for the loss of the first loved one has really receded.

Erich Fromm's book 'The Art of Loving' might not immediately be picked up by bereaved people. Its title suggests that it is concerned only with adult erotic love, and it might therefore give painful, sharp reminders of what has been lost. But the book has a far wider application than that. The section on self-love, especially, from which this passage comes, could be of universal application, and the whole book could be a profound comfort to many who were either brought up or educated into puritanical ideas of duty, denying oneself and serving other people.

In bereavement's adjustment-of-the-focus-of-love process, one of the first positive steps could be to concentrate on self-love. In the bereavement context that means being tolerant of oneself and one's present weaknesses, cherishing and being kind to oneself, and gradually seeking reassurance of personal identity in both emotional and practical ways.

There must be some essential difference, which perhaps someone can tease out, between self-love in Fromm's sense (I would call it self-cherishing) and self-pity. How much self-pity to allow oneself is always a difficulty. Many do find that if they indulge in it very much then they feel more inadequate as well as wrung out with extreme sadness. Maybe these negative results are alone sufficient reason to suggest we try to limit our indulgence if we can. And yet some self-pity is almost our right. No close death is a minor or insignificant thing: we have lost so much, and we do have to adjust almost all aspects of our life so radically.

While it raises no objection to apply the concept of love to various objects, it is a widespread belief that, while it is virtuous to love others, it is sinful to love oneself. It is assumed that to the degree to which I love myself I do not love others, that self-love is the same as selfishness. This view goes far back in Western thought. Calvin speaks of self-love as 'a pest'. Freud speaks of self-love in psychiatric terms but, nevertheless, his value judgement is the same as that of Calvin. For him self-love is the same as narcissism, the turning of the libido towards oneself. Narcissism is the earliest stage in human development, and the person who in later life has returned to this narcissistic stage is incapable of love; in the extreme case he is insane. Freud assumed that love is the manifestation of libido, and that the libido is either turned towards others – love; or towards oneself – self-love. Love and self-love are thus mutually exclusive in the sense that the more there is of one, the less there is of the other. If self-love is bad, it follows that unselfishness is virtuous . . .

These questions arise: Does psychological observation support the thesis that there is a basic contradiction between love for oneself and love for others? Is love for oneself the same phenomenon as selfishness, or are they opposites? Furthermore, is the selfishness of modern man really a *concern for himself* as an individual, with all his intellectual, emotional and sensual potentialities? Has 'he' not become an appendage of his socio-economic role? *Is his selfishness identical with self-love or is it not caused by the very lack of it?* . . .

Not only others, but we ourselves are the 'object' of our feelings and attitudes; the attitudes towards others and towards ourselves, far from being contradictory, are basically *conjunctive*. With regard to the problem under discussion this means: love of others and love of ourselves are not alternatives. On the contrary, an attitude of love towards themselves will be found in all those who are capable of loving others. *Love, in principle, is indivisible as far as the connection between 'objects' and one's own self is concerned.* Genuine love is an expression of productiveness and implies care, respect, responsibility and knowledge. It is not an 'affect' in the sense of being affected by somebody, but an active striving for the growth

and happiness of the loved person, rooted in one's own capacity
to love.

To love somebody is the actualization and concentration of the
power to love. . . . From this it follows that my own self must
be as much an object of my love as another person.

ERICH FROMM

From **The New English Bible**

> For love is strong as death,
> passion cruel as the grave;
>   it blazes up like blazing fire,
>   fiercer than any flame.
> Many waters cannot quench love,
>   no flood can sweep it away;
> if a man were to offer for love
>   the whole wealth of his house,
>   it would be utterly scorned.

SONG OF SONGS 8:6, 7

Here is Donne's famous passage, 'No man is an island'.

Perchance he for whom this bell tolls may be so ill as that he
knows not it tolls for him; and perchance I may think myself so
much better than I am, as that they who are about me, and see
my state, may have caused it to toll for me, and I know not that.
The Church is Catholic, universal, so are all her actions; all that
she does belongs to all. When she baptizes a child, that action
concerns me; for that child is thereby connected to that Head which
is my Head too, and engrafted into that body, whereof I am a
member. And when she buries a man, that action concerns me:
All mankind is of one Author, and is one volume; when one man
dies, one chapter is not torn out of the book, but translated into
a better language; and every chapter must be so translated; God
employs several translators; some pieces are translated by age,
some by sickness, some by war, some by justice; but God's hand
is in every translation; and his hand shall bind up all our scattered
leaves again, for that Library where every book shall lie open to
one another: As therefore the bell that rings to a sermon calls not

upon the preacher only, but upon the congregation to come; so this bell calls us all . . . No man is an island, entire of itself; every man is a piece of the continent, a part of the main; if a clod be washed away by the sea, Europe is the less, as well as if a promontory were, as well as if a manor of thy friends or of thine own were; any man's death diminishes me, because I am involved in Mankind; and therefore never send to know for whom the bell tolls; it tolls for thee.

JOHN DONNE

This passage could at a first quick reading be confused with the Joyce Grenfell verse on page 108, but it has different ideas and a different flavour. It is worth looking at the two together to see which has the closer appeal.

If I should die and leave you here awhile,
Be not like others, sore undone, who keep
Long vigils by the silent dust, and weep.
For my sake, turn again to life and smile,
Nerving thy heart and trembling hand to do
Something to comfort weaker hearts than thine.
Complete those dear unfinished tasks of mine,
And I perchance may therein comfort you.

A. PRICE HUGHES

Isaac Penington was a seventeenth-century Quaker.

The time is at hand wherein time shall be no more; and then whatever had a being in time, shall cease from being so any longer. We must all look to the grave, to the dust; we must all sleep an eternal sleep, when once the last night comes: when we shall bury all our quarrels and contentions, and awake in perfect life and love: and then we shall be, both to ourselves and one another, what now we cannot so much as desire to be.

ISAAC PENINGTON

In his later years Rabindranath Tagore, the great Bengali mystic and poet, tried his hand at writing unrhymed English verses. Here is one such poem.

From Poems

As the tender twilight covers in its fold
of dust-veil marks of hurt and
wastage from the dusty day's
prostrations, even so let my great
sorrow for thy loss, Beloved,
spread one perfect golden-tinted
silence of its sadness o'er my life.
Let all its jagged fractures and distortions,
all unmeaning scattered scraps and
wrecks and random ruins, merge in
vastness of some evening stilled with
thy remembrance, filled with endless
harmony of pain and peace united.

                              RABINDRANATH TAGORE

'A Severe Mercy' is a moving book by an American, Sheldon Vanauken, about his love for Davy, and her death from cancer at an early age. The title comes from C. S. Lewis's description of her death. A friend of them both, in their Christian group in England, Lewis is a kind of guru in the book, giving further depth to their discussions about Christianity, love and death. There is a further extract from 'A Severe Mercy' on page 124.

And yet, amidst the tears and the pain, there was a curious hint of consolation in one thought: the thought that nothing now could mar the years of their love. As he had written to his friend, C. S. Lewis in England, the manuscript of their love had gone safe to the Printer.

He wished for a moment that Lewis were here with him . . . Lewis understood so well, somehow, the nature of loss. Although he was so far away across the sea, Lewis had been his mainstay in this half-year of sounding the depths of grief. He it was who had said that Davy's death was a severe mercy. A severe mercy – the phrase haunted him: a mercy that was as severe as death, a death that was as merciful as love. For it had been death in love, not

death of love. Love can die in many ways, most of them far more
terrible than physical death; and if all natural love must die in one
way or another, Davy's death – he and she in love – was the death
that hinted at springtime and rebirth. Sitting there on the rough
wood of the bridge, he remembered his absolute knowing – something beyond faith or belief – in the moments after her death, in
that suddenly empty room, that she still was. She had not ceased
with that last light breath. She and he would meet again: 'And
with God be the rest!'

SHELDON VANAUKEN

*The extract below is taken from a speech, 'Modern Man facing Death',
which Metropolitan Anthony of Sourozh gave to the Cruse International
Conference on Bereavement following Violence, in September 1983.*

With every person who dies, part of us is already in eternity. We
must, if we love this person, live up to the great encounter of a
living soul with a living God. We must let go of everything that
was small, that was separation, alienation and estrangement, and
reach out to that serenity and greatness, newness and abundance
of life into which the departed person has entered. We should not
speak of our love in the past tense. Love is a thing that does not
fade in a faithful heart. It does not go into the past unless we betray
our love. We must keep our love alive in a new situation, but as
actively and creatively, and more so, more often, than when the
person was with us. Our love cannot be dead because a person has
died. If that is true, our life must be a continuation of theirs, with
all its significance. We must reflect on all that was beauty, and
nobility, in that person, and make sure those around us, and our
surroundings, do not lose anything through the death. This applies
to all families and friends as well as the immediate bereaved, so
that the seed that has fallen into corruption may give a hundredfold
harvest in the hearts and lives of others.

One thing is at the front, with every bereaved person – the sense
of separation, of being left alone. One has to accept it creatively
and to say 'I have a double task to fulfil – the dead person's work
and my own. I must be great for two, reveal integrity for two.'

METROPOLITAN ANTHONY OF SOUROZH

From **Remembrance of Things Past**

It is often said that something may survive of a person after his death, if that person was an artist and put a little of himself into his work. It is perhaps in the same way that a sort of cutting taken from one person and grafted on to the heart of another continues to carry on its existence even when the person from whom it had been detached has perished.

MARCEL PROUST

Remember

Remember me when I am gone away,
    Gone far away into the silent land;
    When you can no more hold me by the hand,
Nor I half turn to go yet turning stay.
Remember me when no more day by day
    You tell me of our future that you planned:
    Only remember me; you understand
It will be late to counsel then or pray.
Yet if you should forget me for a while
    And afterwards remember, do not grieve:
    For if the darkness and corruption leave
    A vestige of the thoughts that once I had,
Better by far you should forget and smile
    Than that you should remember and be sad.

CHRISTINA ROSSETTI

From **an anonymous author**

It is eight weeks, beloved, since you died.
You left the stiffening inert lump of clay
That was no longer you,
And cried aloud in ecstasy
And suddenly I knew
That all that we believed in,
Lived for, told the world,
Had at its smallest count
Some measure that was true.

It is eight months, beloved, since you died,
And out of my aloneness I have woven strength
To build anew;
For all there was of truth in our relationship
Had eddied, grown, intensified,
Till with a clarion call it sounds at the far
   reaches of the world –
There is no death, no separation of the ways
If man to love prove true.

It is eight years, beloved, since you died.
And for eternity a part of you
Is in its essence me.
I know you are, and in that certainty
Is woven all the fabric of my life.
Gone is all sense of urgency and haste;
For all time now, our spirits meet in time.
Loving, we are no longer bound by love;
Heart of my heart, we've set each other free.

For These Once Mine

With you a part of me hath passed away;
For in the peopled forest of my mind
A tree made leafless by this wintry wind
Shall never don again its green array.
Chapel and fireside, country road and bay,
Have something of their friendliness resigned;
Another, if I would, I could not find,
And I am grown much older in a day.

But yet I treasure in my memory
Your gift of charity, and young heart's ease,
And the dear honour of your amity;
For these once mine, my heart is rich with these.
And I scarce know which part may greater be –
What I keep of you, or you rob from me.

GEORGE SANTAYANA

8

Begin again

The things that we learn in the darkness are safely ours for ever.

If the phrase 'begin again' belongs to anyone, it belongs to Margaret Torrie. Perhaps it is almost the motto of Cruse, the National Organisation for the Widowed, which she founded in 1959. It is the title of her handbook for widows. And 'begin again' is what we have to do in widowhood.

In the last paragraph of 'Begin Again', Margaret Torrie suggests that there are 'clearly-marked signposts which, if followed, lead the way to recovery. First there has to be the wish, however transient, to find the way to better things. It is the beginning of hope, that basic ingredient for all life. From there confidence and belief develop, and the certainty that in spite of all evidence to the contrary, good is in us and around us offering support. In such a situation of positive thinking we cease to be dreamers and accept fully our present lot. It is the material from which we are to build our future . . . The remarkable discovery we can make is that love has not deserted us, and that it is available to us now in a new way. Our own willingness to love and to give in the world about us is the secret of recovery and the new beginning.'

There is no quick way. The new understanding and new determination have to come through sorrowing, searching, not finding; and eventually accepting and finding meaning. But slowly, through loneliness, many will discover the quiet value of solitude. Through fearful feelings of separation and insecurity they may discover a new resilience in independence. Through the sensitive friendship and support they have received themselves, they may know how to befriend others more effectively, even to stand alongside other kinds of suffering. This new insight is a most precious gift, often noticed and appreciated by widowed people.

A widower wrote: 'For months I never imagined that life would be good to me again, or that I would even want it to be good. But it is, and I do. My grief has been by far the deepest, most significant thing that has ever happened to me.'

Lord Hailsham sent us a biblical quotation for this anthology. He wrote: 'There is no comfort you can offer to the bereaved more comprehensive than the following':

Are not two sparrows sold for a farthing? And one of them shall not fall to the ground without your Father . . . Fear ye not therefore. Ye are of more value than many sparrows.

AUTHORISED VERSION, MATTHEW 10:29, 31

Here are Lily Pincus's thoughts about the length of time grieving may take. She calls it 'mourning' (see page 4).

We have seen that the course of mourning cannot be predicted because it depends on many factors, such as the relationship between the lost person and the survivor, the circumstances of the death, the external situation, and the inner resources of the bereaved. Therefore, however much we learn about patterns of mourning, they will take different forms with each individual. The precondition for a person to 'complete' his mourning process must be that he is allowed to mourn in his own way and time.

There is no norm for mourning and no norm for adaptation; nor can there be any definite time limit for either. The time mentioned in studies for the various phases and for the total process of mourning is too short to fit the needs of many mourners. One year, comprehending the full circle of the seasons with their birth and death symbols, may be the most meaningful 'objective' period of time for the completion of the mourning process, although I have known mourners who after the loss of their partners suffered from episodes of depression, despair, and regressive setbacks for well over two years and later made exceptionally good adaptations to a new life. Even then, periods of despair and grief as well as searching may recur in special external or internal situations, such as an anniversary or illness.

. . . The mourning process involves the healing of a wound. Once the physical wound has been safely covered by healthy tissue, the process is completed and the patient does well to forget all about the injury. In mourning, however, the cause of the injury, the loss of an important person, must not be forgotten. Only when the lost person has been internalized and becomes part of the bereaved, a part which can be integrated with his own personality and enriches it, is the mourning process complete, and now the adjustment to a new life has to be made.

LILY PINCUS

One cannot fail to recognize the special anguish of bereavement as the result of someone's suicide. The strongest stabs of self-reproach can be unrelenting, and ripples of remorse seem to spread very widely, even affecting mere acquaintances.

I do not know the circumstances of this poem, but those who are suffering greatly after a suicide could perhaps hang on to the thoughts in it.

The Existence of Love

I had thought that your death
Was a waste and a destruction,
A pain of grief hardly to be endured.
I am only beginning to learn
That your life was a gift and a growing
And a loving left with me.
The desperation of death
Destroyed the existence of love,
But the fact of death
Cannot destroy what has been given.
I am learning to look at your life again
Instead of your death and your departing.

MARJORIE PIZER

From The Conquest of Happiness

A man of adequate vitality and zest will surmount all misfortunes by the emergence after each blow of an interest in life and the world which cannot be narrowed down so much as to make one loss fatal. To be defeated by one loss or even by several is not something to be admired as a proof of sensibility, but something to be deplored as a failure in vitality. All our affections are at the mercy of death, which may strike down those whom we love at any moment. It is therefore necessary that our lives should not have that narrow intensity which puts the whole meaning and purpose of our life at the mercy of accident.

BERTRAND RUSSELL

Let the Dead Depart in Peace

Slowly the muddy pool becomes a river,
Slowly my mother's disease becomes death,
When wood breaks, it can be repaired.
But ivory breaks for ever.
An egg falls to reveal a messy secret.
My mother went and carried her secret along,
She has gone far –
We look for her in vain.
But when you see the Kob antelope on the way to the farm,
When you see the Kob antelope on the way to the river –
Leave your arrows in the quiver,
And let the dead depart in peace.

YORUBA FUNERAL SONG

To My Mother

Most near, most dear, most loved and most far,
Under the window where I often found her
Sitting as huge as Asia, seismic with laughter,
Gin and chicken helpless in her Irish hand,
Irresistible as Rabelais, but most tender for
The lame dogs and hurt birds that surround her –
She is a procession no one can follow after
But be like a little dog following a brass band.
She will not glance up at the bomber, or condescend
To drop her gin and scuttle to a cellar,
But lean on the mahogany table like a mountain
Whom only faith can move, and so I send
O all my faith, and all my love to tell her
That she will move from mourning into morning.

GEORGE BARKER

The Intention

Healing is both an exercise
and an understanding
and yet not of the will
nor of the intention
It is a wisdom
and a deeper knowledge
of the daily swing
of life and death
in all creation
There is defeat
to overcome
and acceptance of living
to be established
and always
there must be hope
Not hope of healing
but the hope which informs
the coming moment
and gives it reason
The hope which is
each man's breath
the certainty of love
and of loving
Death may live
in the living
and healing rise
in the dying
for whom the natural end
is part of the gathering
and of the harvest
to be expected
To know healing
is to know that
all life is one
and there is no beginning
and no end
and the intention is loving

MARGARET TORRIE

The Sorrow Tree

The spiritual leaders of
ment in Russia a couple
pictures, metaphors. O
Tree.

When the Hasidic
the most, their spir
that, come Judgen
up all his own p
huge Tree of Sor
found a branch, the,
look for someone else's
preference to their own. In the
own sorrows: they seem more bearable

(partial text from overlapping page:)
122
hopes, to turn away
of submission to P
gate of wisdom.
But passive r
by renunciatio
our own idea
the realm o
bled king
where b
remo
disc
thi

ADAPTED FROM H...

The Life Instinct

God grant that out of suffering,
I take not the easy route,
succumbing to disease.
Let me with prowess rather
fight the fight of resolution,
transcend the agonies and storms:
not faltering – crack.

I'll turn each crisis to solution.

RUPERT STRONG

Perhaps Bertrand Russell's writing is so very rich partly because, as he says himself, 'My intellect goes with the humanists, though my emotions violently rebel'.

To every man comes, sooner or later, the great renunciation. For the young, there is nothing unattainable; a good thing desired with the whole force of a passionate will, and yet impossible, is to them not credible. Yet, by death, by illness, by poverty, or by the voice of duty, we must learn, each one of us, that the world was not made for us, and that, however beautiful may be the things we crave, Fate may nevertheless forbid them. It is the part of courage, when misfortune comes, to bear without repining the ruin of our

ur thoughts from vain regrets. This degree
wer is not only just and right: it is the very

nunciation is not the whole of wisdom; for not
alone can we build a temple for the worship of
s. Haunting foreshadowings of the temple appear in
imagination, in music, in architecture, in the untrou-
dom of reason, and in the golden sunset magic of lyrics,
auty shines and glows, remote from the touch of sorrow,
from the fear of change, remote from the failures and
chantments of the world of fact. In the contemplation of these
gs the vision of heaven will shape itself in our hearts, giving
once a touchstone to judge the world about us, and an inspiration
by which to fashion to our needs whatever is not incapable of
serving as a stone in the sacred temple.

Except for those rare spirits that are born without sin, there is
a cavern of darkness to be traversed before that temple can be
entered. The gate of the cavern is despair, and its floor is paved
with the gravestones of abandoned hopes. There Self must die;
there the eagerness, the greed of untamed desire must be slain, for
only so can the soul be freed from the empire of Fate. But out of
the cavern the Gate of Renunciation leads again to the daylight of
wisdom, by whose radiance a new insight, a new joy, a new
tenderness, shine forth to gladden the pilgrim's heart.

BERTRAND RUSSELL

From **De Profundis**

To regret one's own experiences is to arrest one's own development. To deny one's own experiences is to put a lie into the lips
of one's own life. It is no less than a denial of the soul. . . .

The important thing, the thing that lies before me, the thing
that I have to do, if the brief remainder of my days is not to be
maimed, marred, and incomplete, is to absorb into my nature all
that has been done to me, to make it part of me, to accept it
without complaint, fear, or reluctance.

OSCAR WILDE

Strength

Inside,
I am making myself strong.
I am weaving bands of steel
To bind my soul.
I am knitting stitches of suffering
Into my hands
To make them strong.
I am strengthening my mind
With the warp and weft
Of weariness and endurance.
I am binding my faith
With the bonds of psalms and songs
Of all who have suffered.
In time,
I will be tempered like fine steel
To bend, but not to break.

MARJORIE PIZER

These words are from a crime novel, 'The Tiger in the Smoke'.

Mourning is not forgetting . . . it is an undoing. Every minute tie
has to be untied and something permanent and valuable recovered
and assimilated from the knot. The end is gain, of course. Blessed
are they that mourn, for they shall be made strong, in fact. But the
process is like all human births, painful and long and dangerous.

MARGERY ALLINGHAM

Via Dolorosa

Do not make the mistake
of imagining that you
may go singing
on the Via Dolorosa
neither may you
bear right or left
the way is confined
with little room
for manoeuvre

You will know exhaustion
    kneeling often
    trodden and rough
    and scarred by many feet
    this way is our way
    and may not be shunned
    turned from
    or avoided
    best to go quietly
    with a dogged courage
    knowing that
    one thing is certain:
    There is an end

And when you arrive
    you will find
    that the hill is crowned
    with a living tree
    stretching out
    great branches
    to give you shelter
    and manna there
    and spring water

MARGARET TORRIE

Here is another extract from 'A Severe Mercy', where Sheldon Van-auken describes what he calls the Second Death – the passing of grief.

The train arrived about sunset, and, as I walked up the ascending streets, past old houses, towards the cathedral above, the air was full of golden light. Davy and I had never been in Lincoln, yet now, when I had walked but a short way, I became aware of an extraordinary sense of her presence. I was very peaceful, having her there, if she was. There was no catch in my throat or tear in my eye, just the sense of her presence. And as I walked up that hill, Davy seemed to walk lightly beside me. The sun was setting now. The gold turned to red. Rooks circled, flying home to their nests in the cathedral towers. The great bell boomed for the half hour. The cathedral was rose-red in the sunset. And Davy was beside me. I was tranquilly happy. All was most well.

I did not think of that lovely walk up to the rose-red towers as a farewell, yet perhaps it was. In later times I was to think of it as the last thing *we* did.

In Virginia again, no longer living at Mole End, I found that my tears were dried. The grief had passed. When I drove out to Ladywood, there was no sense of Davy's being there with me, nor any sense that she was in the wind. If I wrote to her – I attempted it but once – I found myself saying 'she' instead of 'you'; the feeling of its being a real letter had vanished. There were no more dreams. It may be that through the evocative power of music, I might have felt a stab of grief, but I had no wish to force it or prolong it beyond its natural term.

This – the disappearance of the sense of the beloved's presence and, therefore, the end of tears – this is the Second Death.

I could not escape the impression that the Second Death was a *withdrawal* – that Davy had withdrawn herself from me. It seemed something more or other than merely a changing psychological state in me. It seemed to correspond to some actuality, some real spiritual event. If, indeed, grief is a *response* to the presence – seeming or real – of the dead, then the end of grief might correspond to some necessary turning away on *their* part. That walk up to the cathedral might have been, in truth, a farewell.

The disappearance of the grief is not followed by happiness. It is followed by emptiness. C. S. Lewis in his letter on eternity quoted me as saying that my love for Davy must, in some sense, be killed – and 'God must do it'. Now perhaps God *was* doing it. And it was, precisely, my earthly love for her – an earthly love that would endure as long as she seemed near – that was being killed. That love had not died when she died – had not died perhaps in *either* of us – and it sustained me in the grief that may have been *our* grief. She had been near to me, it seemed, waking and in dreams – especially in that one incredible dream. I had felt her in the wind. I had rushed from London to Oxford to find her in the misty night. I had walked up the streets of Lincoln with her . . .

Now all that was gone, leaving emptiness. I wanted the grief again, not for itself but for its corollary: the presence that calls it forth. But it is not allowed. There was only emptiness. I was drained of all emotion. My mother, whom I loved, died, and I could not feel anything. Life had no savour. The Second Death, in many ways, is a harder thing than the first, only of course one has no tears for it . . .

The Second Death and Davy's withdrawal towards the Mountains of Eternity – whatever it means – does not of course mean that

I love her any the less, though it is a love without the immediacy of
the flesh . . .

When I myself come to cross that boundary that she has crossed,
I think I shall find her hand and hear her voice first of all.

SHELDON VANAUKEN

The Heart Could Never Speak

The heart could never speak
But that the Word was spoken.
We hear the heart break
Here with hearts unbroken.
Time, teach us the art
That breaks and heals the heart.

Heart, you would be dumb
But that your word was said
In time, and the echoes come
Thronging from the dead.
Time, teach us the art
That resurrects the heart.

Tongue, you can only say
Syllables, joy and pain,
Till time, having its way,
Makes the word live again.
Time, merciful Lord,
Grant us to learn your word.

EDWIN MUIR

From Living Alone

A period in the wilderness, if it serves no other purpose, does at
least help one to get one's priorities in order. The things once
assumed to be essential for one's life, such as the constant company
of other people, society's approval, one's own reputation amongst
those who amount to something in the world's eyes, and the
number of important people one knows seem suddenly to dissolve
like a mist of unreality. It is a revelation in those narrowed circumstances how simple life can be when it is shriven of the accretions
of social usage and conformity. What at first seems to be almost

too unbearable to confront suddenly widens out into a prospect of inner freedom, perhaps the first opportunity to be oneself since one came to self-awareness when one was a small child. It is at this point that one may begin to know oneself for the first time in one's life. The self one knows is, in fact, a central point within, the secret place which is the cornerstone on which the whole edifice of the person is erected.

MARTIN ISRAEL

Christopher Leach's book 'Letter to a Younger Son' is about the death of a child (see page 56) but some of its conclusions could be applicable to anyone.

[Death] can cast us down for more than the necessary period of mourning. It can blight our days, so that we exist forever in that chill, unexpected land. It can whisper to us that life is ultimately meaningless. If what awaits us at the end is our own obliteration, and the same grief we now feel is transferred like a disease to those who love us, what is the point of going on, of ambition, of rearing children who too will one day fail and fall? It can hang like an albatross about our necks; or enclose our hearts in ice; or change us so deeply that even our closest friends turn away. At its worst, death has taken one life; and is offered another.

And yet it can enrich us. We can live for those who have gone. We can pack into our lives that extra time the dead have given us. For they *have* given us time: the expanded moment that comes when we realize that, for us, the blood still moves; the world is still there to be explored and made over; that, for now, this minute, this hour, this day, we are free of pain and hunger; that, though we still mourn in the deepest part of our being, death has liberated us, has made us see the transitory nature of everything; and life, being transitory, is thus infinitely more precious; commanding more attention than ever we gave it when we went on our way, still unthinking children, before death opened our minds, sharpened our eyes; and set us free. . . .

What have I discovered?

I have discovered the ache of loss, the coming of a deeper grief than I thought possible. I have witnessed the extinction of a personality, and have been made to face the continuing certainty that never again shall I see that loved individual. I have discovered the transitoriness of all things; and their consequent worth while they are with me. I have discovered the uncaring nature of the universe; and yet, as a living entity, I am sustained in an attempt to permit me wholeness. I have discovered that men make religions out of their own limited apprehensions of their world; and that, outside their own imaginings, exists a mystery which they can never name, only trust. I have discovered that tragedy need not diminish those who suffer it: that it has a positive aspect; and that, having won through to some kind of angry acceptance, brings a more realistic view of life, and a deeper resonance.

What have I learned?

I have learned what is important. That, faced with the ultimate, things move to a correct proportion. That every day free of pain is a bonus. That there exists in myself acres of my nature which are still undiscovered: one has been opened by grief – what others may be known in the future, sprung by a more disciplined art, or travel, or meetings with strangers? I have learned to be wary: the time that is left is savoured now, dwelt upon, treasured. I have learned compassion: I know what it is to mourn. I have learned, too late in one respect, that I have not cared enough. And now it is too late: for him. But not for you. I have learned the strength of my own creativity: that, called upon, it never fails to respond, and joyfully. It rushes in to heal; and for that I am grateful. I have learned to expect death; and though I resent its intrusion, I grant its cold necessity.

What do I believe?

I believe I share in the making of the universe, perhaps many universes. I am engaged in a stupendous working out of forces, the nature of which I have only the minutest of understanding; and yet know intuitively that I, and even the smallest atom-fizzing rock, are somehow part of an experiment which is in its first, possibly uncertain stages. I believe in life; and my belief is strengthened by death. I believe that somewhere there exists an answer, but that the wrong questions are being asked; or even that no question is needed. I believe it is not what happens to a man that matters, but his opinion of what happens. I believe to laugh at life is better, and saner, than condemning it: the experiment may be the work of a mad scientist, but to die laughing is not a bad way to go.

And I have always believed, in life, the best is yet to come. I cannot speak for the other side, the dark.

CHRISTOPHER LEACH

The letter below was written by a priest to a contessina living in Florence, on Christmas Eve 1513. We can presume she is grieving – whether for her husband, for a dead child, or for someone else (surely one has a real right to grieve for a friend?), we do not know. But the priest is anticipating that Christmas, with all its merriment and festivities, can be a dreaded time for those who are grieving.

Especially in the first year, of course, most widowed people seem to find the two or three weeks immediately before Christmas the hardest: when they actually reach the festival, usually it does not turn out to be as harrowing as they had feared. They get through it, and another major hurdle has been surmounted.

Most Noble Contessina,
. I salute you. Believe me your most devoted servant. The rascal who carries this letter, if he devour them not on the way, will crave your acceptance of some of the fruits of our garden. Would that the peace of Heaven might reach you through such things of earth!

Contessina, forgive an old man's babble. But I am your friend, and my love for you goes deep. There is nothing I can give you which you have not got; but there is much, very much, that, while I cannot give it, you can take. No Heaven can come to us unless our hearts find rest in it today. Take Heaven! No peace lies in the future which is not hidden in this present little instant. Take peace!

The gloom of the world is but a shadow. Behind it, yet within our reach, is joy. There is radiance and glory in the darkness, could we but see; and to see, we have only to look. Contessina, I beseech you to look.

Life is so generous a giver, but we, judging its gifts by their covering, cast them away as ugly or heavy or hard. Remove the covering and you will find beneath it a living splendour, woven of love, by wisdom, with power. Welcome it, grasp it, and you touch the Angel's hand that brings it to you. Everything we call a trial, a sorrow, or a duty, believe me, that angel's hand is there: the gift is there, and the wonder of an overshadowing Presence. Our joys, too; be not content with them as joys, they too conceal diviner gifts.

Life is so full of meaning and of purpose, so full of beauty – beneath its covering – that you will find that earth but cloaks your heaven. Courage, then to claim it: that is all! But courage you

have: and the knowledge that we are pilgrims together, wending
through unknown country, home.

And so, at this Christmas time, I greet you; not quite as the
world sends greetings, but with profound esteem, and with the
prayer that for you, now and forever, the day breaks and the
shadows flee away.

I have the honour to be your servant, though the least worthy
of them.

FRA GIOVANNI

The Future

I walk through the silent town. A breeze is blowing
Snuffed-out candles from horse-chestnut trees.
The unknown is on the air, and I am knowing
Something I cannot recognize, unless

It is a distant prospect of the future, showing
All that is and all that will come to be,
As blossoms of the past are going, going.

NEIL POWELL

Look to this day!

Look to this day! For it is life, the very life of life. In its brief
course lie all the varieties and realities of your existence: the bliss
of growth, the glory of action, the splendour of beauty. For
yesterday is already a dream, and tomorrow is only a vision, but
today, well-lived, makes every yesterday a dream of happiness,
and every tomorrow a vision of hope.

Look well, therefore, to this day! Such is the salutation of the
dawn.

FROM THE SANSKRIT
(Author and translator unknown)

Rebirth

> I am emerging from an ocean of grief,
> From the sorrow of many deaths,
> From the inevitability of tragedy,
> From the losing of love,
> From the terrible triumph of destruction.
> I am seeing the living that is to be lived,
> The laughter that is to be laughed,
> The joy that is to be enjoyed,
> The loving that is to be accomplished.
> I am learning at last
> The tremendous triumph of life.

MARJORIE PIZER

From Living Alone

The removal of a loved companion renders life meaningless, at least for a considerable period, until one has regained one's bearings and begun to see the path ahead. Life that is tolerable must be imbued with purpose to give it meaning. The human mind cannot tolerate meaninglessness, for a meaningless life can assume a quality of non-existence that seems worse than death itself. For death is the great unknown experience which may conceivably open up a new vista of fulfilment, whereas the interminable misery of a mortal life that is purposeless and devoid of growth is something that can scarcely be contemplated in normal consciousness. How can one proceed with living in such circumstances? This is the valley of the shadow of death, cold and featureless, that is mentioned in Psalm 23. Until one knows its contours and extent as well as one does one's native domain, one has not tasted life fully. The end is a changed person, one who lives the transpersonal life, whose perspectives are no longer limited to human objectives but are infused with divine forebodings.

MARTIN ISRAEL

As the Rooks Are

Alone as the rooks are
In their high, shaking homes in the sky at the mercy of winds,
Alone as the lurking trout or the owl which hoots
Comfortingly I have a well-crammed mind
And I have deep-down healthy and tough roots.

But in this house where I live
In one big room, there is much solitude,
Solitude which can turn to loneliness if
I let it infect me with its darkening mood.
Away from here I have an abundant life.
Friends, love, acclaim and these are good.

And I have imagination
Which can travel me over mountains and rough seas;
I also have the gift of discrimination.
High in a house which looks over many trees
I collect sunsets and stars which are now a passion.
And I wave my hand to thousands of lives like this,
But will open my window in winter for conversation.

ELIZABETH JENNINGS

Trying to overcome loneliness

There are many bereaved people who have surmounted the bitterness of being alone, and some who have found rich opportunities in new activities and friendships. Although there is still much to be done in neighbourliness and the provision of help for the bereaved, it is possible in most areas in this country to find an organization or social group that is wanting to know and care for those who are lonely.

For some, loneliness, a-lone-ness, may be the opportunity to experience the quiet joy that can be found in solitude. There are productive activities that can only be practised on one's own. Some have learnt to play an instrument, which might have been an excruciating experience for a marriage partner. Others have passed time catching up on reading and have found it far more enjoyable now that they can read in depth and at leisure rather than in the spare minutes snatched from a busy day. Some have learnt a foreign language, perhaps through radio lessons, while others have used the media to indulge a new or revived interest in astronomy, heraldry, politics or one of a hundred other possible subjects. A number – perhaps a rather surprisingly large number – have turned their minds to meditation.

Two kinds of activity seem particularly to encourage healing of the spirit. The first is any form of creativity. Striving to bring something original into being is a positive personal assertion that life is – after all – worthwhile. Even small creative achievement is balm to those who are weary of the pain of loss and death.

Some have taken up painting or pottery, embroidery, weaving, woodcarving, perhaps going to classes for the first time since they left school. Others have tried their skill with words, writing stories or articles, poetry, a novel or autobiography; they may have joined a local Writers' Circle where they will have found advice and encouragement. . . .

Another sphere of activity, gentle or strenuous as one may choose, which seems to have a special healing quality, is one that brings people in touch with nature: country walks, fishing, gardening, collecting shells or pebbles along a quiet stretch of beach, propagating and caring for houseplants or a herb garden – the opportunities are many and varied. In the closeness to natural and living things – sun, sea, rain and wind, earth and seeds and grass, woods, trees and flowers, bees, birds, butterflies – in the sight and sound and feel of natural elements and growing things, many have found themselves refreshed and at peace.

It is a hopeful, gladdening experience to listen to those who are still rather sad at heart telling of their hobbies, and sharing the quiet joy and precious contentment that they have found in productive solitude.

ELIZABETH COLLICK

On Courage

I sang as one
Who on a tilting deck sings
To keep their courage up, though the wave hangs
That shall cut off their sun.

As storm-cocks sing,
Flinging their natural answer in the wind's teeth,
And care not if it is waste of breath
Or birth-carol of spring.

As ocean-flyer clings
To height, to the last drop of spirit driving on
While yet ahead is land to be won
And work for wings.

Singing I was at peace,
Above the clouds, outside the ring;
For sorrow finds a swift release in song
And pride its poise.

                                              CECIL DAY LEWIS

Vera Brittain's dilemma is the dilemma of many, in one way or another.
The courageous resolve she expresses here is really the climax of her
'Testament of Youth'.

There remained now only the final and acute question of loyalty
to the dead; of how far I and the other women of my generation
who deliberately accepted a new series of emotional relationships
thereby destroyed yet again the men who had once uncomplain-
ingly died for them in the flesh. Up and down the narrow, solitary
roads through Regent's Park, or round and round the proletarian
paths of Paddington Recreation Ground, I walked pondering this
ultimate uncertainty. In spite of myself and the grief for their
unfulfilled lives that no time could diminish, a gulf had stretched
between my spirit and theirs; the world in which at the Armistice
I seemed to have no part had closed in and absorbed me – or was
it, rather, that my own view of my destiny had widened to the
dimensions of its needs?

If the dead could come back, I wondered, what would they say
to me? Roland – you who wrote in wartime France of 'another
stranger' – would you think me, because I marry him, forgetful
and unfaithful? Edward, Victor, Geoffrey, would you have me
only remember you, only dwell in those days that we shared so
long ago – or would you wish my life to go on? In spite of the
War, which destroyed so much hope, so much beauty, so much
promise, life is still here to be lived; so long as I am in the world,
how can I ignore the obligation to be part of it, cope with its
problems, suffer claims and interruptions? The surge and swell of

its movements, its changes, its tendencies, still mould me and the surviving remnant of my generation whether we wish it or not, and no one now living will ever understand so clearly as ourselves, whose lives have been darkened by the universal breakdown of reason in 1914, how completely the future of civilized humanity depends upon the success of our present halting endeavours to control our political and social passions, and to substitute for our destructive impulses the vitalizing authority of constructive thought. To rescue mankind from that domination by the irrational which leads to war could surely be a more exultant fight than war itself, a fight capable of enlarging the souls of men and women with the same heightened consciousness of living, and uniting them in one dedicated community whose common purpose transcends the individual. Only the purpose itself would be different, for its achievement would mean, not death, but life.

To look forward, I concluded, and to have courage – the courage of adventure, of challenge, of initiation, as well as the courage of endurance – that was surely part of fidelity. The lover, the brother, the friends whom I had lost, had all in their different ways possessed this courage, and it would not be utterly wasted if only, through those who were left, it could influence the generation, still to be, and convince them that, so long as the spirit of man remained undefeatable, life was worth having and worth giving. If somehow I could make my contemporaries, and especially those who, like myself, had once lost heart, share this belief; if perhaps, too, I could have children, and pass on to them the desire for this courage and the impulse to redeem the tragic mistakes of the generation which gave them birth, then Roland and Edward and Victor and Geoffrey would not have died vainly after all. It was only the past that they had taken to their graves, and with them, although I should always remember, I must let it go.

> . . . *Under the sway*
> *Of death the past's enormous disarray*
> *Lies hushed and dark.*

So Henley had written: and so, with my eyes on the future, I must now resolve.

VERA BRITTAIN

For Those Who Weep

I have a pearl
to give to you who weep
whose beauty's born
from simple life
and fashioned out of pain
it fills a mandala
with space to breathe
and gently gathers light
it is not struck from rock
or circled like a diamond noose
to bind you by
but free and perfect
grew unknown
where nature turns invading pain
to beauty and delight

So hold it fast
and catch the spread of sunrise
in the single point of light

MARGARET TORRIE

These are the concluding words of 'A Way to Die', the book that Rosemary and Victor Zorza wrote about their daughter Jane, who died from cancer when she was twenty-five.

When we went back to Washington at the end of the summer, we became aware of a change in ourselves. We were thinking far more than ever before about what really matters in life, about feelings, about the more abiding human values, about people – people as individuals. Jane talked of all these matters in her last weeks, and she made them more real to us than they had been. She also took pleasure in passing on her more cherished possessions to her friends. She gave a lot of thought to it. She liked to see them walk away with something she had given them, after they had said goodbye.

'I don't need a "thing" to remember Jane by,' said one of her friends. 'Jane taught me how to make bread. Whenever I make bread, I think of her.'

Before she died, we had talked of how people live on in what they do, in their actions, in the memories of those they have influenced. That was how Jane hoped she would live on. And she will.

ROSEMARY AND VICTOR ZORZA

Acceptance

There is an end to grief
Suddenly there are no more tears to cry
No hurt nor break now
But mute acceptance of what will be
Knowing that each move for good or ill
Must fit the whole
Past comprehension
Yet trusted in the design
This way lies peace

BRENDA LISMER

Index of sources and acknowledgements

The compiler acknowleges with gratitude the courtesy of the following companies and individuals in permitting the use of copyright material. For Bible versions, see under general heading 'Bible'. Page numbers appear in **bold** type.

African's prayer, an, *see* Carden, John

Allingham, Margery, *The Tiger in the Smoke*. Chatto & Windus 1952. Reproduced by permission of Curtis Brown Ltd, London on behalf of the estate of Margery Allingham. **123**

Andrewes, Lancelot, prayer from *Preces Privatae*. **62**

Anonymous, deathbed prayer from the Gaelic. Author and translator unknown. **62**

Anonymous, 'Give them rest', from an early Christian prayer. **59**

Anonymous, 'It is eight weeks, beloved', quoted by George Trevelyan in *Magic Casements*. Coventure 1980. **114**

Anonymous, 'Let the Great Shepherd Lead'. **65**

Anonymous, passage from ancient Sanskrit. Author and translator unknown. **130**

Anonymous prayer ('Thy love is like a great sea'), quoted by Elizabeth Goudge in *A Book of Comfort*. Michael Joseph 1964. **64**

Anonymous prayer 'We seem to give them back'. Bede Jarrett O.P. (1881–1934) described finding it and was probably its first public user, but his source is unknown. **60**

Anonymous, verses sometimes entitled 'The Weaver'. **39**

Anonymous, 'Western Wind', *c.* A.D. 1500. **1**

Anthony, Metropolitan, of Sourozh, extract from a speech made at the Cruse International Conference on Bereavement following Violence, Sept. 1983, and summarised in *Bereavement Care* journal, Winter 1983. © Cruse Bereavement Care. **113**

Apocrypha, the. Extracts from the Authorised King James version of the Bible and Apocrypha and the Book of Common Prayer 1662, which is Crown Copyright in the United Kingdom, are reproduced by permission of Eyre & Spottiswoode, Her Majesty's Printers, London. **69, 74**

Auden, W. H., *Collected Shorter Poems*. Faber 1966. By permission of Curtis Brown Ltd. on behalf of the estate of W. H. Auden. **26**

Sjöberg. Faber 1964. Reprinted by permission of Faber & Faber Ltd. **61**

Hardy, Thomas, *Collected Poems*. Macmillan 1925. **35, 43**

Hasidic teaching, *see* Sorrow Tree, The

Henley, William Ernest, *A Book of Verses*. David Nutt 1912. **29**

Herbert, George, *The Temple* 1633. **94**

Hesse, Hermann, *Reflections*. Translated by Ralph Manheim. Jonathan Cape 1977. Used by permission of the estate of Hermann Hesse and the translator. **95**

Hogg, Quintin, from *The Devil's Own Song*. Hodder & Stoughton 1968. Reproduced by permission of Hodder & Stoughton Ltd. **99**

Holland, Canon Henry Scott, passage attributed to. **86**

Hopkins, Gerard Manley, *Poems*. Oxford University Press 1967. **27, 70**

Hughes, A. Price, passage attributed to. **111**

Indian Christian, Meditation by an., *see* Carden, John

Israel, Martin, *Living Alone*. SPCK 1982. **89, 96, 126, 131**

Jennings, Elizabeth, *Collected Poems*. Macmillan 1967. **10, 29, 48, 132**

John Chrysostom, St, from *Homily I, on II Corinthians*. Translator unknown. Quoted in *Death: a Book of Preparation and Consolation*. ed. Barry Ulanov. Sheed & Ward, New York 1959. **52**

Julian of Norwich, Mother, *Enfolded in Love*. Translated by members of the Julian Shrine. Darton, Longman & Todd 1980. **61**

Kavanagh, Patrick, *Collected Poems*. Macgibbon & Kee 1964. By permission of Mrs Katherine Kavanagh. **19**

Keats, John, from 'Endymion'. **87**

Kushner, Harold, *When Bad Things Happen to Good People*. Pan 1982. **38, 40**

Leach, Christopher, *Letters to a Younger Son*. Dent 1981. **56, 127**

Leney, Nora, *In a Lifetime*. JMR Publishing Co., New York 10012, NY 1975. **15**

Lewis, C. S., *A Grief Observed*. Faber 1961. By permission of Faber & Faber Ltd. **28, 105**

Lewis, C. S., *Letters to Malcolm*. Geoffrey Bles 1964. **75**

Lewis, C. S., *The Pilgrim's Regress*. Dent 1933. **13**

Lismer, Brenda, poems 'Sharing' and 'Acceptance' previously published in *Cruse Chronicle*. © Brenda Lismer, c/o Cruse Bereavement Care. **20, 137**

Lively, Penelope, *Perfect Happiness*. Heinemann 1983. **14**

Lowell, James Russell. **52**

MacDonald, George, *Annals of a Quiet Neighbourhood*. Hurst & Blackett 1867. **99**

Russell, Bertrand, from 'A Free Man's Worship' in *Mysticism and Logic*. Allen & Unwin 1976. **121**

Russell, Bertrand, from *The Conquest of Happiness*. Allen & Unwin 1975. **118**

Santayana, George, poem 'For These Once Mine'. Printed by permission of Bucknell University Press, Lewisburg, Pa. USA. **115**

Sanskrit, from the, *see* Anonymous

Scannell, Vernon, poem from *Selected Poems*. Allison & Busby 1971. **23**

Schiff, Harriet Sarnott, *The Bereaved Parent*. Souvenir 1979. **48**

Scott, Diana, poem from *Bread and Roses*. Published by Virago Press Ltd. 1982. This collection copyright © Diana Scott 1982. **51**

Selden, John, from *Table Talk*. **21**

Shakespeare, William, *Macbeth*. **23**

Sidney, Sir Philip, prayer supposed to have been written by. **65**

Silkin, Jon, poem from *Selected Poems*. Routledge & Kegan Paul 1980. **49**

Sitwell, Edith, from poem 'Eurydice' in *Collected Poems*, Macmillan 1957. Published by permission of David Higham Associates. **xiv**

Song of Songs, *see* Bible: New English Bible.

Sorrow Tree, The, story from traditional Hasidic teaching. **121**

Stoppard, Tom, from *Rosencrantz and Guildenstern are Dead*. Faber 1968. Reprinted by permission of Faber & Faber Ltd. **4**

Stott, Mary, *Forgetting's No Excuse*. Published by Virago Press Ltd 1975. Copyright © 1973 by Mary Stott. **31**

Strong, Rupert, *Poems*. Runa Press, 2 Belgrave Terrace, Monkstown, Co. Dublin, Ireland 1974. Printed by permission of the author. **121**

Tagore, Rabindranath, *Sadhana*. Macmillan. By permission of Macmillan, London and Basingstoke 1913. **80**

Tagore, Rabindranath, from 'Gitanjali' from *Collected Poems and Plays*. Macmillan. By permission of Macmillan, London and Basingstoke 1936. **12, 15, 64, 67**

Tagore, Rabindranath, *Poems*. Macmillan. By permission of Macmillan, London and Basingstoke 1923. **112**

Tatelbaum, Judy, *The Courage to Grieve*. Heinemann 1981. **9, 25**

Tennyson, Alfred Lord, 'In Memoriam' from *Collected Poems*. **18, 92**

Thomas, Dylan, *Collected Poems*. J. M. Dent 1952. **30**

Thompson, Sally, poem 'Ox-Eye Daisies, Loweswater, One June Day'. Not previously published. © Sally Thomson c/o Cruse Bereavement Care. **24**

Torrie, Margaret, *Begin Again*. Dent 1970. © Margaret Torrie. **116**

Torrie, Margaret, from *Selected Poems*. Cruse Bereavement Care. Margaret Torrie. **91, 92, 120, 123, 136**

Vanauken, Sheldon, *A Severe Mercy*. Hodder & Stoughton 1977. Copyright © 1977 by Sheldon Vanauken. Reprinted by permission of Hodder & Stoughton Ltd. **112, 124**

Vaughan, Henry, from poem 'They are all gone'. **67**

Waddell, Helen, *Medieval Latin Lyrics.* Constable 1929. **42, 102**
Waley, Arthur, from *Seventeen Old Poems.* Allen & Unwin. By permission
   of Mrs Alison Waley. **11, 26**
Waley, Arthur, 'At Night I Dreamt' from *More Translations from the
   Chinese.* Allen & Unwin 1919. **42**
Wallbank, Susan, poem 'Death makes philosophers of us all'. Not pre-
   viously published. © Susan Wallbank, c/o Cruse Bereavement
   Care. **12**
Warner, Sylvia Townsend, *Letters*, edited by William Maxwell. Chatto &
   Windus 1982. By permission of the author's literary estate and
   Chatto & Windus. **13**
Warner, Sylvia Townsend, from *Twelve Poems.* Chatto & Windus 1980.
   By permission of the author's literary estate and Chatto & Windus.
   44
Watkins, Vernon, from the poem 'Peace in the Welsh Hills'. By permis-
   sion of Mrs Gwen Watkins. **91**
Whale, John, 'Better 9 plus G than never'. *Sunday Times*, 22 April 1984.
   © Times Newspapers Ltd. **93**
Wilde, Oscar, *De Profundis* 1905. **122**
Wisdom of Solomon, *see* Apocrypha
Wordsworth, *The Poetical Works of Wordsworth.* Oxford University Press.
   88

Yoruba funeral song, *see* Beier, U.

Zorza, Rosemary and Victor, *A Way to Die: the story of Jane Zorza.* André
   Deutsch 1980. **136**

Every endeavour has been made to trace the copyright owners of each
extract. There do, however, remain a few extracts for which the source
is unknown to the compiler and publisher. The publisher would be glad
to hear from the copyright owners of these extracts and due acknowledge-
ment will be made in all future editions of the book.